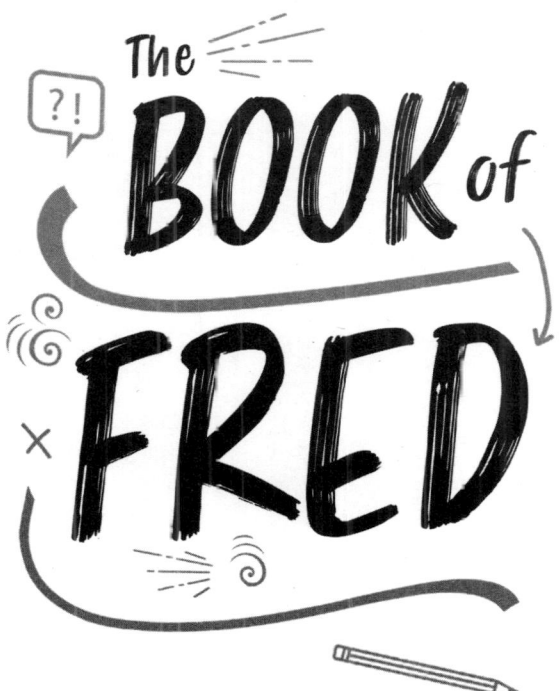

EXCLUSIVE SIGNED EDITION

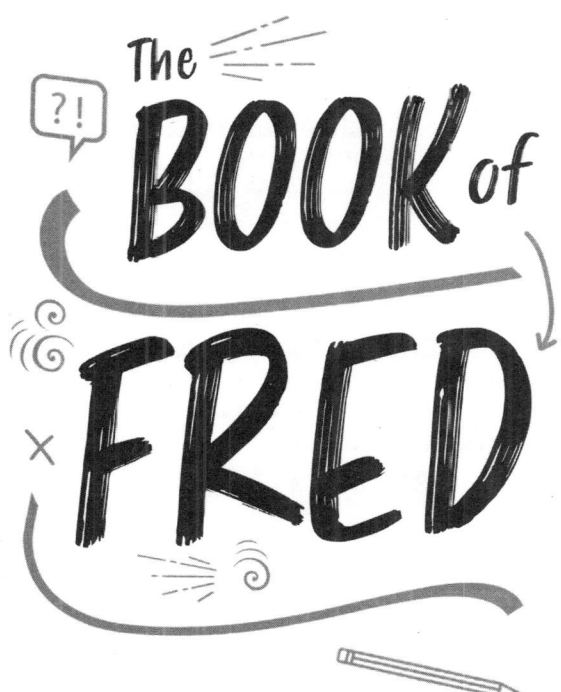

FREDDIE FLINTOFF

First published in the UK by Blink Publishing
An imprint of Bonnier Books UK
4th Floor, Victoria House,
Bloomsbury Square,
London, WC1B 4DA

Owned by Bonnier Books
Sveavägen 56, Stockholm, Sweden

Hardback – 978-1-788-704-88-5
Trade Paperback – 978-1-788-704-89-2
Ebook – 978-1-788-704-90-8

All rights reserved. No part of the publication may be reproduced, stored in a retrieval system, transmitted or circulated in any form or by any means, electronic, mechanical, photocopying, recording or otherwise, without prior permission in writing of the publisher.

A CIP catalogue of this book is available from the British Library.

Typeset by IDSUK (Data Connection) Ltd
Printed and bound in Great Britain by Clays Ltd, Elcograf S.p.A.

1 3 5 7 9 10 8 6 4 2

Copyright © Andrew Flintoff, 2021
Lyrics on page 4 © Gerry Cinnamon

Andrew Flintoff has asserted his moral right to be identified as the author of this work in accordance with the Copyright, Designs and Patents Act 1988.

Every reasonable effort has been made to trace copyright holders of material reproduced in this book, but if any have been inadvertently overlooked the publishers would be glad to hear from them.

Blink Publishing is an imprint of Bonnier Books UK
www.bonnierbooks.co.uk

To Grandpa

CONTENTS

Introduction		1
Chapter 1	Growing Up	9
Chapter 2	Confidence	33
Chapter 3	Work	65
Chapter 4	Friendship	121
Chapter 5	Failure and Success	145
Chapter 6	Fame	163
Chapter 7	Money	207
Chapter 8	Mental Health	233
Epilogue	Home	257
Acknowledgements		267
Index		269

INTRODUCTION

I've been listening to a lot of Gerry Cinnamon over the last 18 months. If you don't know who Gerry is, you should check him out. He's this mysterious Glaswegian singer/songwriter. You hardly hear him doing interviews or pushing himself like a lot of musicians or bands tend to do, but he's generated this incredibly devout following up and down the UK.

I've been watching footage of his gigs and his fans go absolutely nuts when he's onstage. YouTube is awash with mad clips of punters climbing whatever they can scale, hoisting themselves higher than the rest of the throng while at the same time singing every single word back to him at the tops of their lungs and generally just losing it completely. Every time I see them, I can't help thinking I want to be right in the middle of it, part of that crazy choir, getting stuck right in.

There's one particular track I play all the time at home, called 'Canter'; it's huge. On a very simple level, I love the melody and it's a song you can easily sing along to. But the lyrics are so special because they feel like a manifesto or a mission statement for people like me. It's optimistic and a great way to start the day, it's almost a mantra: 'This is the beginning of the rest of your life/You better start graftin' 'cause you're running out of time . . .'

That's how I start every day, thinking it's the beginning of the rest of my life and I need to put a shift in. Though I do I feel a bit guilty that I've got a one-year-old son dancing in a highchair listening to me singing: 'You know it could be a canter/If you were just a wee bit less of a wanker'. Possibly some questionable parenting going on there but it's fine, he's still oblivious.

There's a line in 'Canter' about it not being about playing the game, but about how much you care about playing the game – how much it really matters to you. I've mulled that one over a lot, in relation to my own life and my career in cricket too. There's no question I cared about being a cricketer, but could I have cared even more? Could I have looked after my body better? If there's one thing I know it's that there are no simple answers in life – I am where I am now because of the way life played out. While I'm not sure I'm someone who believes 'everything happens for a reason', and I'd never want to re-live the pain of the injuries or the disappointment of having to retire early, everything that's happened did get me to the place I'm in right now.

INTRODUCTION

That's the thing about great songwriting – it's specific but it's sort of universal too. It touches a nerve and makes you think about things in your own life. I'm a married father of four who has played sport at elite level and I now find myself hosting one of the biggest shows on telly. On paper it might sound like I've got a pretty decent handle on things and I've found a lot of the answers but the truth is, like everyone, a lot of the time I'm still trying to make sense of it all. On the other hand, I've definitely not been a stranger to sticky situations over the years, but I feel like I have a perspective and life experience now that I definitely didn't have when I was younger!

What I'm trying to say is that I'm not one to tell anyone else how to live their life. What I've done in these pages is take the chance to look back on some of the experiences I've had and to ask myself what I've learned along the way. There's plenty that I wish I'd known when I was younger, so maybe talking about some of it here will help you.

I've come to realise that a lot of what makes me feel happy, or maybe it's more like content, boils down to a sense of belonging and being part of something bigger. I always feel like I need to belong to something. I always wanted to be popular, but I'm not sure I've achieved any of these things, because I still don't know how to behave. There is something in me that wants to conform and be known and easily identified, but at the same time, I like solitude and just being at home with my family.

It's hard to retrace your steps and know exactly why you did what you did all the time but ultimately, the important thing is to know who you are and where you've come from. That reminds me of another of Gerry's songs, actually, an anthem called 'Diamonds in the Mud'. He's singing about the South Side of Glasgow, but for me, it could be about my hometown of Preston, as it really resonates with what I was feeling and experiencing where I grew up in Lancashire. The track is all about the mix of emotions associated with a place that still manages to bring a smile to your face when they pop up in your head – particularly when you are feeling low. It's also about travelling far from home but nothing really compares to those familiar streets of your upbringing; it's about the people who you might think are rough but are actually 'diamonds in the mud'.

That lad Gerry, he really is a storyteller. His experiences have made him the poet, the writer, the musician he is. Every word he's committed to song comes from his experience growing up in Glasgow and that resonates with me. I really am obsessed. That's the problem with me: when I lock on to something, I'm done. That's it – I'm completely hooked.

It's good to get into stuff, to really care about the things that mean something to you, but I've definitely learned that

INTRODUCTION

life is about balance, that you need to look after all aspects – your career, your family, your mates, your health. Work is important but you've got to make time for the people closest to you. That said, if you are dialling it in and spending your time concentrating on your golf swing or taking your partner away every third night, chances are you'll find yourself in hot water at work.

I've got a pretty simple approach to things and being laid-back, without a plan written down, has worked for me. With a bit of luck, I'm somewhere around the halfway point of a good life on this planet. I've had some amazing experiences – and some pretty weird ones too, it has to be said. You'll struggle to find another book on the shelves dropping names like Jeremy Beadle in the same pages as former PM John Major. I've ridden the highs of elite sport and felt the bump when I've crashed back down to earth. I've left a job I loved, changed careers and had to learn a whole new set of skills. Honestly, it's sort of exhausting when I think about it, but my point is, I've learned a lot. And not just from being a cricketer or being on TV. Just as many – maybe more – of my most important lessons have come from working in Preston Woolies or a man called Pete who lived on the edge of Old Trafford's car park. Anyway, I've written about it all here so you can judge for yourself.

So here you go, *The Book of Fred*. Like everything in life, take it with a pinch of salt and at some points, a JCB digger might be required for my views, but that's the best thing about other people's opinions – take as much or as little notice as you like. As we start to emerge from all the lockdowns, it has been incredible. Working at the cricket over the summer of 2021 and seeing the crowds back has given me a huge lift, it has been such a strange time for everyone.

OK, I'm also off to stalk Gerry Cinnamon round all the festivals he's going to be performing at this summer. It's not that long until I'll be able to see Gerry for the first time, which is mad considering how long I've been listening to his songs now. He'll be fed up of me by the end of this year. I can already imagine him thinking, *There he is, that big cricket prick is in the crowd again.*

CHAPTER ONE

GROWING UP

'It is possible to come from nowhere and get somewhere.'

A Cricket Education

I was 15, in the fourth year at Ribbleton Hall High School, Preston, and I was playing cricket to a good standard. Things were really beginning to happen for me.

I was playing for Lancashire Under 15s against Yorkshire and I got 40-odd runs. There was this old boy called John Savage and he said, 'Do you wanna play for the second team tomorra?' I didn't know what he meant so I told him he'd better have a word with my dad. Before I knew it, I was playing in the reserves the next morning in a three-day game against Glamorgan at Old Trafford in me England U-15s cap.

Then, at the end of the week, I was given £60 made up of crumpled-up fivers and a tenner in a brown envelope. 'What's that?' I said and was told it was my match fee. I also got 10p a mile for my dad for his petrol every day. I just thought, *This is bonkers!* They were giving me money for playing cricket! I didn't realise you could get paid, I just thought you played for the fun of it and so I couldn't get my head around the fact it was an actual job.

I carried on playing for Lancashire in the reserves and I signed my first club contract for £2,500-a-year still at 16. Now I found myself surrounded by professional cricketers and people I had seen on the telly, it was mental. I was taking some huge steps into a man's world, but I was still really immature. Although excited to be there, I was a naïve teenager with a lot of potential and not much of a clue how to fit in. Oh, and no pubes!

None. Nothing. I was about 20 before I had proper hair on my legs. I wouldn't shower with the rest of the lads because I was self-conscious about it. I'd been around men's dressing rooms since I was about 11 with my dad's team, Dutton Forshaw, so I knew what pubes were and I was very aware that I didn't have 'em. I knew some of the kids I played with had 'em, like Gareth Batty, who was the same age and went on to play for Yorkshire, Surrey and England. I remember seeing his ginger pubes the previous year and wondering why I didn't have any. That became a bit of a thing because everyone noticed I wasn't showering but they left me alone. No wonder – I was really young.

There was a telly in the corner of the dressing room. One day, an advert came on – Joanna Lumley was promoting Müller Vitality yoghurt and all the lads were talking about her. You don't need me to paint the picture for you. I'll never forget it. The coach, John Stanworth, asked me, 'What do you think, Fred?' and I just replied innocently, 'I'd lick that.' Genuinely, I was talking about licking the lid of the yoghurt. It was probably the first time I got a good laugh in the dressing room and I didn't even understand why because I was too young and wet behind the ears.

The thing about dressing rooms is that they're a zoo. I couldn't have told you this was what was happening at the time but I was finding out where I would belong in the food chain. Figuring out those unspoken rules and going along with the laughter (even though I had no idea why it was so funny), as well as saving myself from embarrassment in the shower as a slow developer, helped me survive through my early career. It established me in a sport full of big personalities. Looking back, it has probably done some damage, too.

My first away trip with the team was a few weeks after the Joanna Lumley incident I mentioned. We were playing at Middlesex, travelling down on the team coach, leaving from Old Trafford. I turned up in my blazer, shirt and tie thinking that was the done thing. There nice and early, I was sat at the front of the bus – the model pro. The other players started turning up and getting on the coach.

Ronnie Irani was still at Lancashire and a big fella called Ian Austin. They both showed up with a big Esky (portable cooler) filled to the brim with beer, which they put down at the back of the bus. I'd never had a drink before – until that day. By the time we got to Stoke 45 minutes away, I was pissed!

I was five cans down and had a tie around my head when we arrived in London. But it was pouring with rain. We were rained off for three days.

The dressing room was packed with characters. They came in all shapes and sizes but it didn't take long to work out who the big personalities were. You know the ones – the loudmouth, the prankster, the violent one, the quiet one, the arrogant one . . . There were a couple of lads in particular who immediately stood out as genuine mischief-makers. Chris Brown played for Lancashire second team in the 1990s, he was some man. Most of the lads in the team at that time seemed wild to me.

There was another lad, whose nickname was Les the Liar, tenuously based on Manchester United goalkeeper Les Sealey. He was like the fantasist fella in Peter Kay's *Phoenix Nights*, who was always like, 'You'll never guess who I met the other day – Robert De Niro!'

I spent most of the day with Les the Liar and then in the evening I was in tow with Ronnie Irani and Ian Austin. Ronnie left Lancashire in 1993 and went to Essex for 13 years. We played against each other and we didn't really get on. He was a Bolton lad and I always felt he had a chip on his shoulder about not making it at Lancashire. It's funny because he used to dish out quite a lot of shit in my direction but since we both retired, we get on great and he's actually a really good lad. Professional sport can do that to you – the desire to win at all costs can damage a lot of relationships.

Anyway, I spent three days getting pissed for the first time in the company of professional sportsmen and I was in the bookies, all the pubs, the nightclubs. I hardly had any money at all, but what little I did have, I bet on the horses. It was wild and that was my introduction to senior cricket in England. And then I had to go back to school. I was getting £30 a day – £20 for my evening meal and an extra tenner for lunch because we were rained off. It wasn't enough boozing to ruin me with a hangover, but it definitely made me realise there was a consequence to all-day drinking.

The headmaster asked me to give a talk to the school assembly and I had to say, 'I can't do it.' There was absolutely no chance. What was I going to say? We didn't play any cricket at all.

'Good morning, everyone. I turned up at the ground, sat at the front of the bus, had my blazer and tie on. Then, before the coach had even started moving, I had begun drinking, dipping into a crate of cold beer whenever I fancied one. I was hammered by the time we reached the hotel and I didn't play cricket in London. No, we had a great long lie-in every morning, we got up, went to the bookies, then we were in the pub by mid-afternoon. When we got hungry, we visited some lovely restaurants and by evening, we were in nightclubs in Gerrards Cross. Would you like me to tell you what karaoke songs the players performed, sir?'

No, I don't think that report would have reflected well on the duty of care shown by a professional cricket organisation. Here's the thing, though – it was bloody brilliant! It might sound flippant, and yeah, I was too young for most of it really, but I learned so much in those few days.

Looking back, I may have missed a trick because actually getting up and saying that in assembly might have got me a bit more respect and credibility, rather than everyone thinking I was a saddo for going down to the Big Smoke to play cricket. At my school, cricket wasn't a popular or cool sport to play. There was also a little bit of jealousy knocking around because I'd gone to London, hadn't I? That was seen as a bit Billy Big-Time among some folk. One of my mates, Wayne, was 40 when he came to my wedding in London and it was the first time he'd ever been. He was a Preston lad and had just no inclination at all to go down south. Then, when he finally ventured there, it blew his mind.

I'd already been burnt with assemblies when I was 11, so I knew I'd be doing myself no favours at all if I agreed to get up there. By then, I'd already been playing for Lancashire under-11s for three years and the headmaster, Mr Stones, a really nice fella, said, 'I'll give you a fiver if you get a 50.' In

1987, that was big money. I got my 50 but the fiver hadn't materialised. Next thing, he's calling me up in front of assembly. I can remember this so well. He handed me this fiver in front of everyone but as much as I wanted the cash, as it was happening, I knew how much trouble the crumpled blue note was going to cause me. I got so much hassle for it – I had a massive target on my back because I had some money in my pocket and the spotlight on me. It's funny how that stuff sticks with you. For weeks afterwards, I was battered with 'teacher's pet' taunts.

After the boozy, gambling madness of the Middlesex trip, I knew I didn't want that sort of attention on me again. What was I going to get up and say, anyway?

On Tour

The first time I went abroad was on tour to South Africa for a month when I was still 15. I got a month off school, which was a result – it was lovely. After that, it felt like I was constantly on tour every year until I was 31. Though my mum wouldn't let me go to Australia to play club cricket when I was 16 as she said I was too young to go to the other side of the world for most of the winter. A month was a good experience in South Africa but Australia was a different commitment entirely. I'm definitely not complaining – I have to make that clear – but it's not what you could describe as a normal life. I was sacrificing a lot of things like knocking about with my mates at the park, which doesn't sound like something significant but to me it was a big part of life that I missed out on. But at least it was keeping me out of other trouble.

I remember being on a plane for the first time and everyone clapped when the plane landed. I was so young, I thought that's what always happened on flights, acknowledging the skill of the pilot with a round of applause. It took me years to realise it was only in certain parts of the North and Scotland where that happened, so when I eventually flew with England, the lads from the South thought I was mental when I started clapping when we reached our destination.

When I was 17 I went on an end-of-season tour of Guernsey. After the Middlesex away experience when I was at school, I'd gone back to drinking Coke. I could neck it and I would do all the player fines with cans of pop but I'd just end up so gassed, it was unreal. I got a hundred in one of the games in Guernsey, which helped me massively. Then, afterwards, someone passed me a pint of Guinness when the team were playing drinking games. I shouldn't have been drinking at all, I was only 17. I necked the pint of Guinness and it was so much easier than doing a pint of Coke. Then I did another one. And another. About ten pints in, I had an epiphany. It was a dangerous realisation: *I'm quite good at this*.

Everyone was bemused but at that moment I felt like I

was accepted. Rightly or wrongly, it gave me huge confidence. Suddenly I had become a competitive drinker. It was a dangerous clash of ability and competitive spirit: I wanted to win at everything and drinking became another thing I had to be the best at.

When I think back to the drinking, it scares me a bit. I thought it really helped me and, with the benefit of time and perspective, it actually did help me early on in my career. I was in a room with men and in those days there was a drinking culture within cricket – you'd have at least a few pints after every single game. I broke into the first team way younger than my friends at the time, so I was often a lot younger than everyone else in the team. Keeping up with the drinking was my way of showing I was fitting in, that I was part of it and I belonged.

It gave me some standing at that point in my life but of course I now know that it really hindered me later on in my career. I think if I'd said I was teetotal and wanted to have a protein shake or some electrolytes, the start of my career might have been very different. Then again, I'd be lying if I said I didn't enjoy almost all of it. But the booze could have been a part of why I retired at 31 with all the injuries I was suffering – I think about it all the time.

As a 43-year-old man I'm now questioning all those lessons learned in dressing rooms, starting from when I was just a kid. I'm pretty sure I've been 'un-learning' things as the years go by and I'm convinced my career in professional cricket would have been so different if I could apply what I now know. They say 'youth is wasted on the young' and that couldn't have been truer for me. Perhaps though, some young sportsmen and women will take some of my mistakes, wayward antics or silly decisions on board and make some better calls.

The Exorcist

As a kid, I used to sleepwalk and I was scared of the dark – I still am. I really struggle with it but only inside a house for some reason. Outside, I'm fine. Every night when I was young, my mum would have to lie with me until I fell asleep. I would wake in the night and I had been sleepwalking. My dad used to work nights at British Aerospace in Preston, so he would come back and find the front door wide open, which, looking back on it, must have been pretty worrying for him as a parent. I woke myself up once when I was ringing my mate Martin Hilton's doorbell in the middle of the night, then I'd run home. I think what started it all off was watching the film *The Exorcist* when I was far, far too young.

Martin lived four doors down and all the kids who lived around us were good pals. Everyone knew each other back then – diagonally across from us were the Smiths, Liz and Dave, they had six kids. Next door to them was a guy called Barry. We would clean the Smiths' car for a bit of pocket money and

Barry said if we cleaned his car, we were welcome to go in his house and use his VCR to watch some videos. (Videocassette recorders were big news back then. My dad used to put tape over the display on ours because we got burgled four times when we were kids and he was convinced it was because they could see the lights on the display from outside on the street.)

Anyway, we washed Barry's car and went into his house. There were probably about eight of us in there when he went out. We watched *Rocky* and then *Raiders of the Lost Ark*. Then someone found a copy of *The Exorcist* and most of the kids decided to leave – except for me and Martin Hilton. Fucking hell! I was on pills two weeks later for nightmares and I've been scared of the dark ever since. I was only ten years old. If my dad had found out we had watched *The Exorcist* at Barry's house then I don't think he would have been kicking about our street much longer!

Peer pressure was massive when I was growing up. Imagine if I'd just said 'no' to watching *The Exorcist*? I genuinely think my life might have played out differently – it left such a big mark on me. At night, I would be whistling through the streets, comfortable in dark rooms on my own, but because Martin Hilton was watching it, I had to watch it too.

If I could pass on one thing: keep an eye on that peer pressure your kids will face. I know only too well that it was the reason I made some bad decisions as a kid.

When you are in the eye of a storm growing up and there might be a bit of bullying or you're just trying to find where you fit in, you can learn resilience, which plays out later in life, but only if you don't let it overwhelm you. It can also be the loneliest existence you can imagine.

I didn't grow up on a council estate but we were surrounded by five or six of them and each one had a gang, each had their reputation and they all went to the same school. It was bedlam. I used to hang around the shops and I was nervy about it because there were always a lot of hard people knocking about. Every day, I went to school not knowing if I was going to have my head kicked in or get involved in some confrontation, someone calling me 'faggot' for playing cricket. But, hard as it was, I wouldn't swap it for anything. I experienced harsher stuff than I ever did in my cricket career and those experiences are so important in your development.

The kids I was around were always talking about weed, acid and LSD at the time but I knew nothing about it or what it was. I'd nod along, but I didn't have a clue. It just wasn't on my radar – I wanted to play sport and everything else went over my head. The only time I was with those people was from 8:20am until 2:50pm and I wouldn't see them outside of that because I'd be off to cricket or helping my mum with her job. Or I would watch *Dallas* on UK Gold at 3pm when I got in.

Every lunchtime at school we would go to the chippy and

GROWING UP

then head round to my mate's to eat them. I didn't know it at the time because I was a bit naïve but his brother was definitely a drug dealer. The place stank of weed but I just didn't know the first thing about it all. People would be coming and going all the time and we'd be sat there watching *Home and Away* while all this was going on around us.

Then when I was about 15, my older brother's mates became my mates too. We all used to go to the social club together to play pool. My mum and dad will be horrified with what I'm about to share: I think I could have been in the back of a nicked car with some older lads. To this day, I still don't know if they were joyriding – it was only after the event it dawned on me. I really hope I wasn't. I didn't properly realise what was going until I got in the back of the car. My mate Martin turned up to pick me up with some other lads, so I just jumped in the back without asking any questions.

It was a bit out of character for Martin; he just showed up and told me his mate had a car, which triggered something in me – I knew he wasn't telling the whole truth. I shouldn't have got in it, but these lads were a bit older and were planning to go to Kirkham to meet some girls. Weirdly, it sticks with me because I was really into Queen at the time. I loved a bit of Freddie Mercury and Queen and I remember it blasting out. It was just awful, a truly terrifying experience. If it hadn't been for the comfort blanket of the Queen songs, I might have cried.

I look at my life now, the people I knock around with, and when I think about where I came from, it does surprise me. It's lucky we survived experiences like that and also, turned out to be decent, law-abiding human beings.

Champagne Supernova

At 16, I got a job at Woolies on the music counter and I was allowed to play whatever I wanted in the shop when I was working. I genuinely loved it because I was really getting into my music at the time. It felt like music was really exciting back then. Oasis's debut album *Definitely Maybe* came out in 1994 and had a big influence on me. For working class lads from the north west, like me, it felt like we were taking over the world and the band just seemed like all the lads I grew up with.

The access I got to music working in Woolies was such a significant part of my teenage years. I really got to know music inside out around that time because I was unpacking records, playing them in the store and then listening to the lyrics all through my shifts. The job also gave me a disposable income, which meant I could go to different clubs and concerts.

One of our favourite venues was The Ardwick in Manchester – it's the O2 Apollo now. We were going to The Ardwick to see loads of gigs around then. I loved Ocean Colour Scene, Paul Weller – I'd go with my brother Chris because he was massively into it. If there's one thing I could have been other than a cricketer, it would have been a musician. Some days, you would want to be a proper frontman – leading from the front, giving it the big 'un. Other days, I'd think, *I'm more of a crooner, me.* Just sauntering around. I think swanning about would be my skill. I spend a lot of time travelling around on my own and I've got to admit my mind does wander, imagining life as a lounge singer.

I always think about what I was learning about music back then, without even realising it was an education. *The Elvis Presley Essential Collection* was one album that has stuck with me – so much so that I ended up performing 'Suspicious Minds' at cricket initiation ceremonies, though I never thought one day I'd sing it on national telly, which happened in 2010 on *A League of Their Own*! I even ended up singing it onstage in Battersea with Sir Elton John in 2006 at my testimonial!

I must admit, I enjoyed hiding behind that Elvis persona. It gave me licence to be flamboyant and show off. As Andrew Flintoff from Preston, I'd struggle to stand up and perform a song at karaoke. But if I could dress up as Elvis and mimic him, I somehow made it work. When I got all the gear on and performed the song on *Cricket AM* on Sky in 2007, it felt like a big moment for me on TV. You might say it's a metaphor for the difference between me and the character of Freddie Flintoff – you can really come out of your shell if you have the cape to put on. In cricket, I could be the bold and powerful Fred. A bit of an alter ego, it helped me find that aggression and the will to win that made all the difference on big occasions.

I used to sell Noel Gallagher's CDs in Woolies and I can still see all the boxes rammed with copies of *Definitely Maybe*. I remember unpacking those boxes, listening to all the songs on the album and going to see the band soon after. It still blows my mind that now I actually know him to say hello to. Thanks to some weird quirk of fate and a career in cricket, I've had the chance to sit with him for hours, drinking at Manchester City.

One night, sitting at the Etihad with my dad, Hacienda DJ Mike Pickering was hanging about – I remember stacking his CDs on the shelves of Woolies too. Another night, about 5am, we ended up with my dad and Noel in the Radisson RED. Dad was just chatting away with Noel like he'd been a neighbour in Preston. As much as he was playing it cool, he loves Oasis and he knows all the songs though. Those moments in life where worlds collide stick out for me. There are certain times in your life, and it doesn't happen to me much, where you have an out-of-body experience. I was so lucky to be there at the Radisson RED with my dad having a night out like that with Noel.

My first big concert was Oasis at Maine Road in 1996. To go from selling Noel's albums to being sat drinking with him? It just goes to show that it's possible to come from nowhere and get somewhere. I've talked to Noel about it on those nights out. I was in Woolies in the 1990s and, before Oasis, he was working for the council as a groundsman.

Community

When I was growing up, Dutton Forshaw C.C. was the beating heart of family life. My dad was the backbone of the place and I rode on the coat-tails of his passion for everything leading up to a Saturday match day – from practice in nets to the preparation of the ground and the fundraising nights. For us, it was everything. More than just a weekend, it was a massive part of life. My brother, my nan and grandpa, my mum, my Auntie Ennis and Uncle Ted, we all felt like part of the fabric and furniture of the place. Dad would help at the ground, he'd be up a ladder fixing a sight screen while my mum would be making the teas.

That experience was so important in my life – the commitment and sense of camaraderie, mucking in and being selfless about supporting the club. It was great to see all these volunteers contributing to the running of the club and how it was the focal point of so many of our lives. It's something I would urge everyone to seek out and sample; the sense of community was really special and brought a lot of people with a common passion and goal together.

Back then, there were some great players and even bigger characters involved on the pitch as well. There was a family called the Patels, who I still see now. I grew up playing with another fella, Mal Dyer, who is like this mythical character from the West Indies. He could hit the ball further than anybody you've ever seen in your life. I'm sure the Flintoffs and our wider family made their mark on a few people, too.

Through taking me along to his club, my dad introduced me to this incredibly diverse world of people from different backgrounds and, hopefully, Rachael and I are doing the same with our kids now. It's such an important aspect of growing up, to be completely integrated as a society, and sport is such a key tool in achieving just that.

Any sporting team is so much more than just the people on the pitch. A club is the product of so many people's efforts. It takes a lot of enthusiasm, hard work and dedication from everyone, not just the players. I might have picked up some of my bad habits through dressing room culture, but I was also really looked out for by a lot of people in the cricket community when I was young and just starting out. And they taught me some really important lessons.

I moved out of home when I was 16 because I had to get to Manchester to play professional cricket for Lancashire and I was still too young to drive. To start with, I lived in a house on the edge of the car park at Old Trafford with the groundsman,

Pete. It was the only way I could make it work at the time and felt like a completely natural decision to move in with him during the winter season. My mum wasn't keen for me to spend my winters in Australia at that age. So during those months and the off season, I was kept on to work at the club and earn my keep where I was needed. The club asked Pete if he would take a lodger and I'm so glad he agreed, it was a big part of my life.

Sadly, Pete's now dead, bless him, but when I knew him, he was a man about town. A big part of my life at that stage, he knew anyone and everyone. He was perceived as this angry, grumpy fella and on the outside, he could give that off, but I'd got to know him really well during that spell. I lived with him for a good few months, probably six in total. I'd get the train home on a Friday afternoon and Mum and Dad would take me back on the Sunday.

The first Sunday I was dropped off, Pete took me to this rough pub around the corner, The Quadrant, in Manchester. It was near enough to the cricket ground to be our local. I remember him saying, 'Alright, we're going for a pint,' on the first night I moved in. We went into this pub and it seemed reasonable enough. All his mates were there – an unlikely bunch, you might say. There was a bit of everything going on. I was looking around the pub and Pete had all sorts of characters next to him and they're all having a good chat. I'm 16, from Preston, and this was all new to me. It seems crazy now to think that was an unusual scene but it was pretty rare back then. There was all sorts of stuff going on in this pub – it was full of faces and characters. Pete seemed to know everyone, it was brilliant to be around and to be introduced to so many people from all walks of life.

Pete asked, 'Do you want a drink?'

'I'll have a pint of Coke,' I said.

He replied, 'You can't have a Coke in here, son. What do you really want?'

So, I went on to have about five or six pints of lager. All the lads had well and truly peaked and at 10:30pm, Pete sent me home. It was only a five-minute walk home, both of us trudging back in silence, then straight to bed when I got in. I say 'trudging', I might have been a bit unsteady on my feet compared to Pete.

Next day, I was expected to report in to the offices for the working week at 8:30am. Same drill every week: went home Friday, came back Sunday. One Sunday, Pete wasn't in when I got back so I set off for the pub. I walked down and some of Pete's mates were there. They called me over and I sat down with these lads and then this fella came limping in past us and went up to the bar. Legless, all wobbly, he was in a right pickle. He had bruises on his head and he said, 'Oh, fucking hell! I've just been run over.'

It was a gang-related thing, apparently. He went on to tell us more of the story. 'Yeah, the coppers came and ran me over. Get me a brandy.' So there I was, sat with a fella who's just been run over by the police and we're drinking brandy.

At 10:30pm on the dot, the door opens. It's Pete, pointing at me: '*You*, home! Now.'

It might sound daft but those experiences were really important to me. They taught me how to handle situations, how to speak to people, how you should react – and, more importantly, how you shouldn't. Never underestimate how crucial that broad experience of life and different kinds of people can be.

Pete was a respected man – I suppose in some ways because he was so well connected. He was like Mr Old Trafford and he knew everyone. If you needed a bit of help, you'd go to Pete. But he just treated everyone so well and completely equally. Whatever background you came from, he wasn't judgemental. If you had a problem, he would front it out and he would stick by you. He was protective – of his mates, of people he liked. It was a lot to do with how much he cared about Lancashire and the club.

He was just a good man to be around.

Through working in the offices at the club and living with Pete, I picked up how important it was to take care of the simple stuff that costs nothing. Good manners in particular.

Saying 'good morning' to everyone helps you to get to know them all on first name terms. Whether it's the kit man, the tea lady, the parking attendant or the chairman, whoever it may be, treat everyone with the same level of respect, how you would like to be treated yourself. That gave me an insight into everyone at Lancashire.

I was working, but I was learning so much more.

I started off in accounts and really struggled there. Then I worked in the ticket office. I ended up running the club shop with Joy, who was the wife of the dressing room attendant, Ron Spriggs – they were a lovely old couple. I was so frightened of Ron, he was a stern guy before you got to know him. He was feared, but when I got to know his missus, our relationship changed and he turned out to be an amazing fella.

I think doing all of those jobs whilst I played for Lancashire meant a little bit more because sometimes, you'd think, I'm a player, *I'm a professional,* but having the experience of the other jobs at the club made it even more special. It was a privilege to have this chance and then I realised that behind the scenes, those people were probably more passionate for the club, even more enthused about what I was doing than I was. Without them, I wouldn't have that platform to perform. We were all in it together. It also made me feel like I'd found another home: I belonged at Lancashire and it was all down to the great people who worked in and around the club.

CHAPTER TWO

CONFIDENCE

'There are times all throughout life when you have to stand up for yourself.'

Awkward

This is a weird one and I think it's a hang-up from when I was young and still at school but all through life, I've never really been confident around other people.

I'm a bit weird, I've got quite a lot of quirks and people who know me will tell you I can be hard work to get close to. I've always struggled with familiarity and letting people in. It's not easy to make friends with me. That's why I don't see many people and I don't keep in contact a lot because I always think people don't like to be around my awkwardness. I don't really know if people like me or not – it's just how I feel and the mood I sense.

I get really insecure about myself with people I don't know very well. I've got a really small group of friends I'm comfortable with and anything outside of that, I feel vulnerable. It's mad, because when it comes to confidence as a sportsman, at times I've had this single-minded, unwavering confidence in that arena. I remember when I was about 16, we had a meeting at Lancashire to talk about our aspirations. A lot of the lads had already realised an ambition in representing the county. I remember the way people looked at me when I told the room I wanted to play world-class cricket – I wasn't afraid to vocalise it at all, I wanted it known.

I genuinely believe I could have played for England at 17 years old – I think I was better at 17 than I was at 20. My temperament was excellent at 17; by 20, things were beginning to change with all the attention I had. For starters, I was about four stone lighter and I didn't have a load of baggage around my neck at 17. I was just this fresh-faced lad who was really unsure of himself in everything other than sport. I suppose in a lot of ways, at that age, I was a fearless cricketer – I just wish I'd had more confidence back then to be me off the field too.

I went to a notoriously rough school but I wasn't a rough kid. I wasn't a fighter and I wasn't ruthless until it came to winning at sport. I actually liked a game of chess and to watch *Coronation Street* on TV, but my temperament was totally different with sport. I really liked cricket and where I grew up, that was the equivalent of being Billy Elliot. At school, I couldn't really be myself or at least that's what I felt. From the age of six, I was playing under-14 cricket, then from nine or ten, I was playing men's cricket so I found I never really had the chance to be myself among my peers, either. Then, when I was playing professionally, I wanted to play the part of someone else – to have an alter ego. In some ways it was a relief because inside I was this insecure person but I always found coping mechanisms. This lad from Preston, who was scared of the dark, wouldn't survive if he was himself – I was very aware of that from an early age.

I don't know if that's part of the reason I was so nervy around people. I was always convinced they didn't like me and I still struggle with that. I don't know where it stems from. Perhaps because I was a bit different at school, I ended up doubting everything. But as soon as I got a cricket bat in my hand, nothing else mattered. I could walk out into any arena not knowing what was going to happen, but I was so comfortable knowing I had a chance to do something special – it gave me huge confidence.

My family and friends give me this huge sense of belonging, which I need. They give me a reason to do what I do and put myself through a lot of it. I couldn't jump off cliffs or make a fool of myself onstage, if it was just for me. But I'm not doing it for me, I want to provide for my family and make them proud. They provide the motivation which helps me summon the confidence to do things, they are my purpose. Almost every day I find myself in a predicament where I'm facing challenges – in a weird way I am always out of my comfort zone.

It's tiring, but I've not been found out yet, nothing has gone really badly. My pal Rob Key always said that to me, 'When it all goes horribly wrong, can I be there please?' It keeps me pushing. One day I fear I will run out of energy, but in the meantime, my family and friends are the catalyst for everything.

Scraps

I remember my first ever fight. If I close my eyes right now, I can see Lee Head, pinning me down by the shoulders and hitting me hard in the face. We were four years old in the yard outside class and he was a bit of a rough kid. At breaktime we ended up having a scrap and somehow he got on top of me. Although I was stronger than him and I could move him about a bit, I didn't have that fighting instinct – it just wasn't in me to use the natural strength I had to hurt him.

That day, I decided to retire from fighting. I wasn't very good at it, I didn't like it and every school I'd been to, my mum and dad had been governors. I was petrified of getting in trouble – and I still am! I've always hated it when I've upset my mum, but my dad was strong, with big hands.

There was this one kid, he gave me a rough ride all the way through school. He was small, but he hit me a good few times and for no particular reason that I could fathom. It didn't hurt that much so I didn't hit him back. As I've said, I just didn't want to – I don't have it in me to hurt someone like that. I didn't get it when other people did when we were younger. Tall and strong, I was always scared about what damage I could do to someone if I really let myself go. He punched me in the face and by not retaliating, I think I made it worse for him because I was fine.

But there are times in life when you have to stand up for yourself, one way or another, and learning how to do that is important. You don't want to get into a scrap but sometimes as a young lad, a bit of physicality is hard to avoid. When I was about 16, me and Paddy, who went on to become my best mate, were thrown in to play against the Lancashire second team. Being totally straight about it, the lads we were up against weren't nice lads. From our perspective, they were swanning around with an arrogance that never matched the talent. Off the pitch, they would also give it the big one when they were out and about. Now I love dressing room humour and the mickey taking, but these lads were just plain nasty. They would jump on any tiny insecurity, picking up on anyone's faults, but not even in a funny way. We took that as a motive, an incentive to show them up, so when I went out batting with Paddy, we were always on a mission.

They would be firing stupid comments at us, really childish stuff, but when it's co-ordinated with a pack of them, it could break weaker players. It's so fresh in my mind, when Paddy said, 'Are we having this?', I was less confident than he was about putting up a scrap so I didn't know what to say. He just said, 'Well, I'm not having it.'

He would go past them for a run and whack them on the ankle, leaving a mark to let them know we weren't going to take it – and it worked.

We established ourselves as lads not to be messed with.

* * *

My dad, Colin, is a big lad. When you see us together, it's fair to say the apple didn't fall far from the tree. He's always been very protective of his family and us kids. A couple of times when I was younger, it kicked off when I was playing cricket. I remember a game at Preston when I was only 11, but playing at under-18 level. The coach of the opposition told his bowler to aim his delivery to hit me on the head. It was at a time when we had no helmets and barely any protection.

Helmets were only really worn on telly during international cricket. I used to bat in a cap and never gave it a second thought when I was growing up. There was always a bit of niggle with Preston, everyone wanted to beat them, so we often found things would get a bit lively.

It was getting into the evening, the light was failing and the wicket was not the best. This guy was telling them to bounce me, so they kept doing it. It wasn't happening to anyone else. The helmet thing was never enforced and it was dangerous, especially because I was so young.

He was shouting instructions over and I knew my dad

wasn't having any of it. He was confident I'd be able to handle what they chucked at me but imagine for a second someone telling an 18-year-old to throw a ball at an 11-year-old's head? No wonder he was angry. I know he had a stern word with the coach and needless to say, he piped down – he always had my back.

When we were growing up and we were all at home together, we never heard Dad swear. The older we got, the more we started to understand that at work, he was an entirely different animal. One of our best mates, Lee Robinson, ended up working with him and if anything ever got back to us about Dad at work, he'd have a right go at Lee and he would immediately fall into line. He has an authority about him that commands respect.

When I was about 20 and my brother Chris was 23 or 24, we went to a sportsman's dinner with my dad. We took him out in Preston afterwards and went to the nightclub, Tokyo Joe's, where I was a bit of a regular around that time. I'd been having a problem with a bouncer who worked there. All the other lads on security were sound with me, but there was this one lad who was becoming a real issue for me.

So, in we went – me, Chris and my dad – and as soon as we were in, this fella was eyeballing me, watching my every move. Nothing happened inside the club but as soon as we were walking down the street for a curry, we happened to bump into him again. We were having a laugh, just joking about, all three of us a bit pissed.

This bouncer walked past with one of his mates and just at the point we're joking to each other, he interrupted us, having a go with the classic line deployed when starting a fight, 'What did you fucking say?'

As me and Chris started squaring up with him, Dad just pushed us both aside and went nose-to-nose with this guy, saying, 'Have you got a problem, mate?'

This bouncer lad just replied, 'Why?'

My dad was right back into him with, 'I'm their dad. I asked if you've got a problem?'

This fella just turned and walked away as if he was trying to look like he wasn't bothered. My dad always had our back.

Suddenly, I'm the same age my dad was when that was kicking off outside Tokyo Joe's. It's not a million miles away from where I'll be walking down the Deansgate in Manchester with my boys, Rocky, Preston and Corey, and the same thing will probably happen with us! It's frightening even writing that down.

* * *

After I retired from cricket in September 2010, I was trying to find ways to replicate the thrill of playing in front of a crowd. I've always loved boxing and I was also really keen to get myself in seriously good shape, so we came up with the idea of making a documentary about the dedication required to become a pro fighter. I'd read about the actor Daniel Day-Lewis training so hard for his movie *The Boxer* (1997) that he was good enough to be a contender. So, I decided to give it a go. I won my only fight against the American heavyweight Richard Dawson in 2012, but I actually hated it. For months I was getting beaten up in sparring. I got absolutely nothing from hitting other people. It might sound mad, but I actually preferred getting hit or taking a punch to see what I could take – it was probably some kind of self-harm if you look into it.

Though getting punched in the head might have been unpleasant, it was nothing like what I went through with my knees and ankles while playing cricket. Pretty much every day of my career, I played in pain. I was getting injections all the time, taking painkillers to get me through games and training. Looking back, I was having a howler but in some warped way, I enjoyed it because it gave me a sense of survival. I was always thinking, *I can get through this*, which made it even better when I was doing well. In the brief moments when I felt right physically, it didn't feel the same when I was winning because it was easier.

It might sound a bit primal, but there are moments in life when you have to put a marker down. It may be something as simple as showing people what your values are and when the line is crossed, you say something. Or it could be something physical, where you need to stand up for yourself and show you can be assertive, as much as the anticipation before something like that is terrifying. Even if it doesn't go to plan, you've shown what you stand for and you can be proud of that.

A Scottish Viking from Preston

I might still be an awkward sort of lad in many ways but as I've grown older, I've definitely learned that important lesson that confidence comes from knowing who you really are and finding a way to be comfortable in your own skin.

For me, something that really helped was completely unexpected. In 2020, I made a documentary with former footballer, now writer and broadcaster Jamie Redknapp in which we learnt about our family history. *Who Do You Think You Are?* had been a really successful series on the BBC and Ant & Dec were commissioned to make something similar but based on DNA analysis as well as historical records to trace their ancestry. *DNA Journey* did really well, so ITV came to me and Jamie to go through the same process.

I've spoken about depression and some of the battles I've had in my life. I can get into my own head at times. I've spent hours, and a lot of money over the years, trying to find out what was going on in my head – and for some reason that *DNA*

CONFIDENCE

Journey really helped things fall into place. I would never have considered before making that programme how helpful it is to understand who you are in a genetic sense. Listening to the experts who worked on the show and appeared on camera explaining the longer version of how you had entered the world and how your family came to exist in the first place was a grounding experience. You can buy DNA kits online which give a breakdown of your DNA in terms of family history through geography and it's something I'd encourage everyone to do. I discovered I'm part Scandinavian, part Scottish and part Lancastrian. So as far as I'm concerned, I'm a Scottish Viking raised in Preston! It's a combination that probably explains why I was pretty good at drinking . . .

I had this idea that I was very English, I'm from Preston and the North and that was about it, really. Initially, I wasn't sure about doing the show as I didn't want to find out I was from a long line of bad people – though maybe that would have explained a few things! It was more than a TV show, it was like a lottery of life. What were our six numbers? What was in the big pot? And once you find out, you can't then *un*-know again. It was a nerve-wracking experience.

Turns out my great grandad Albert Flintoff was a massive character. He was working in the Co-op for ten years in the 1920s and got done for having his fingers in the till. That was just the start of it. Albert was also renting cars but then selling them on. The cars would never go back. It was a bit embarrassing. After that, the old rogue was also declared bankrupt after another of his business ventures went horribly wrong. He then bought a newsagent's and sweet shop, yet another spectacular failure, not least because he was selling things for less than he was buying them for. It was embarrassing hearing that on the show – especially with Redknapp sitting there, chuckling away. His family were heroes – he was being smug about his great, great grandad being a hero miner from Yorkshire. Then we found out his other great grandad robbed half of Liverpool, the greatest robbery since January 1991 when Liverpool FC signed Jamie from Bournemouth for £650,000! But you can't deny that he was a resilient fella, Albert, he kept having a go, which has definitely manifested itself in me over the years. When I watched the show back, it felt like I was quite harsh on old Albert, but looking back on it, the poor fella had been through the wringer.

I've had some spectacular failures and I keep coming back, too. There's a good chance some of that came from Albert. I don't mind having a go and failing, but I genuinely think not trying is a crime. That's one of the biggest things I can shout from this book – you've got to have a go in life. Albert made a pig's ear of things, but I'd like to think he just wanted to make people happy. What you can say about him is he never gave up.

CONFIDENCE

At the end of the show I found out he had fought in the First World War, joining up when he was 18 years old, then finding himself in the middle of the Battle of the Somme. You only need to have turned up for a couple of history lessons at school to realise just how horrific that experience would have been. He was under heavy shelling for seven days, which must have been hellish to say the least, before being sent home with shell shock because the effects were so severe. Because I've had my own battles with mental health, I feel that I can sort of get a sense of what he must have gone through. Not that it really compares – I wasn't up to my knees in mud, blood and devastation.

Albert was awarded the Victory Medal for his services. Finding all this out completely changed my opinion of him. When I first heard his story, I thought he was a rascal, but it all made sense when you understood the price he had paid in war. No wonder he was making irrational decisions and mistakes – he was suffering from what we now call PTSD (post-traumatic stress disorder).

I also learned about a Scottish relative called Sandy Tait, who played for Preston North End and then moved to London, where he captained Tottenham Hotspur. The production team took us to the Tottenham stadium to tell us about this and it was so funny seeing Jamie's face as we waited to find out which one of us had a famous footballer as a relative.

The whole experience of finally knowing the vast majority of my DNA was from Preston made me happy to an extent I wasn't expecting. Now I know that I'm from the place I love, from the place I keep getting drawn back to, and there's a security and comfort in that. Mix that north-west in with a bit of Viking and my love of Scotland and I'm happy with that!

Some of the historians on the show walked me through the Viking history of northern England – they loved Preston, apparently. I learned that the Vikings came across to Scotland for a bit, headed south via York, popped into Lancashire before heading over the Irish Sea to conquer Ireland. When they got there, the Irish were a bit tougher than they anticipated, so they were sent packing to Lancashire. On the road back to York, they followed the River Ribble, thinking it'd lead to Yorkshire, but when they got to Preston they thought, *No point going back any further, we're staying here. We've found Valhalla.*

So the Vikings camped on the banks of the Ribble, at Cuerdale – just by a pub I used to drink in, actually. Back in 1840, some local builders found one of the biggest hauls of Viking treasure in Preston, which the experts believe had been there for a millennium. It was thought the treasure consisted of 8,000 coins from the reigns of Ethelred, Alfred and Edward the Elder, along with large ingots of silver, bracelets, bridle bits and rings, making up to 1,000 items, with some of the coins dating back as far as AD 855.

I'm retelling a history lesson I received recently, so apologies if any of it is a bit wide of the mark. I took the historian's word for it, but look where that's getting us in the world right now – just assuming stuff we are told is true. It'll do for me, though, and this is a book about life, not a historical manuscript, so let's crack on.

I've always wondered about my genetics, my DNA and my ancestry. I believe the older you get, the more inquisitive you are about what makes you tick. Not just the psychology, the genetics and heritage are interesting too. I'm clearly a big bloke, as is my dad, but the blond hair isn't something you would associate with Lancastrians. The Viking revelation was something that triggered all sorts of thoughts about my life, though – and that spirit of competition and aggression in sport.

The never-say-die attitude was definitely something that Vikings had. They were known for scrapping against the odds. Ten would take on 50 without thinking about it and at times, that's how I've felt in my career – there is a deep-rooted sequence of DNA in me somewhere.

More than Money

When I played for Lancashire, I was representing a place I loved, the place I was from. Playing for England gave me exactly the same feeling but I really only realised this consciously –

and how much it meant to me – when I took the opportunity to sign for an Indian team in the Indian Premier League in 2009. The tournament was played in South Africa that year because of local elections in India, which probably paid a part in my identity problem with them.

We moved to Dubai and the plan was to earn some IPL money tax-free for a few years to set us up for life after cricket. My knees were shot and, being totally honest with myself, I sort of knew I probably wasn't going to be playing for much longer. After India, I would move on to play in Australia for Brisbane. But I played three games in the IPL and I didn't enjoy it. I was stood there playing for Chennai Super Kings and my heart just wasn't in it.

Test cricket, international cricket, that's like *Coronation Street*, you know what I mean? That's the thing that everyone remembers. It's tradition and matters to people. The IPL was like *Love Island*. It happens every year, you get people coming and doing it and making a name for themselves, and then they disappear.

The people at Chennai Super Kings were amazing – the owners, the players and everyone involved. But standing there in a yellow kit in South Africa with a team I didn't really know, playing for a place that I'm not from? I didn't have that emotional attachment and that was a massive part of what made me tick as a player. It was a really significant moment in my life when I realised that money wasn't the main motivation for me to play cricket, it wasn't what made me want to win – I had to feel that I was playing for something more than money.

Peacock

I don't go to that many industry dos as chatting to loads of people I don't really know isn't my thing but one of my favourite events to attend is *Attitude* magazine's annual awards. If you'd told the lads I was knocking about with in Preston when I was a teenager that it would be one of the best nights out, Lord only knows how they would have reacted back then. But you enter that party at *Attitude*, it's a room full of people who are just having a great time being themselves. It feels like a celebration of who you really are and that epitomises everything I believe in.

All everyone wants to is to be comfortable in their own skin and I think in every walk of life, if you're not true to yourself, you'll eventually be found out. But on the other hand, that can be really hard sometimes. And I think there's something old-fashioned about this country that makes you portray what you think you should portray. Even the most confident among us (which is definitely not me) feels pressure to behave in a certain way or show off or act how they don't feel on the inside.

I know when I'm peacocking and acting all exuberant or confident, when that's not actually how I feel. If I'm meeting a production company or I go for a new job, I have to be that person that they want me to be. While I'm doing it, I know I'm doing it and I can hear myself so clearly in my head, searching for a laugh. Then I question the authenticity of their laughs: am I actually funny or are they playing a sycophantic game to flatter me? I'll be in the car on the way home and I'll be dissecting what's just happened, wondering if they really thought I was a tit. Why did I say that? Why did I mention something like that? It's the same every time.

In early 2021, I did a run-through for this new game show. I came out of that feeling awkward because you're throwing everything at it, though there's an element of having the confidence to know some of the stuff is shit and ride through it. It's a pilot, so it's not going to be polished and perfect, and you know there's an edit so you have to trust they'll keep the good stuff in and remove the rubbish. It doesn't stop you dying inside as you're doing it and then having to reference an awful gag to the room – I get round it by making myself the butt of the joke.

It was something I learned growing up from lively dressing rooms. Any insecurity about your dress sense, the way you spoke, your car, your family, it would get highlighted and hammered. It goes back to that brutal second team at Lancashire – players would jump on weakness. But if you own those things yourself, folk have nowhere to go. The most famous example was when I was getting all the criticism for my shape and I played out of my skin and battered Zimbabwe at Old Trafford. A reporter asked me about my performance and I said, 'Not bad for a fat lad.'

Ego

Now, ego's a funny one as it's often used negatively, as the bad extreme of confidence, but it's more complicated than that. Everyone has an ego to a certain extent and it's used as a bad word. I disagree with that because to play a professional sport, to appear on TV, to do most things at a high level, you need an ego. The issues are when it gets out of control – that's when it becomes problematic. I have absolutely no qualms in saying I have an ego, of course I do – I've got a bloody alter ego! If I didn't, I couldn't play cricket in the way I did. I couldn't do the TV stuff the way I do. But I think it's a help rather than a hindrance.

Historically, English cricket has always had an issue with underperforming on the big occasions and I think I know why. Everyone speaks about all these great players from the eighties. I believe it was actually the worst time in English cricket when it came to winning. The teams they had then, there was no excuse for them not to win – they had the talent.

In the nineties, when I started playing, I was in the dressing room with some of the best players we've ever had. Fair play to Mike Atherton, I've had my ups and downs with him, but he was a genuine team player. Darren Gough was a special player and the heartbeat of the side, but some of the others – they seemed to have agendas and insecurities and that led to underperforming.

In my opinion, all the selfishness surrounding cricket was the reason we didn't win anything. So many programmes have been made about cricket in the nineties and why it was so bad. There was talk about players being selfish, putting their personal position ahead of the team. Under Vaughany, we had a good run and we beat everyone because we were actually very good. But then, as soon as the shit hit the fan, it all reverted back to the dark days of the eighties and nineties. To be truly great, you need togetherness, team spirit and a bond you can only build beyond cricket.

I think for the first time Eoin Morgan's side have cracked a puzzle that no one else could. England in one-day cricket have always been crap. We've beaten sides on our day, but always ended up on the wrong side of history. Suddenly, we've got a bit of consistency and we're probably the best side in the world in one-day cricket because you've got to be selfless to win. That's the attitude Eoin's brought to the side, where these lads are playing for each other and they're reaping the rewards.

Competition

I have a funny relationship with competitiveness. In many ways I'd say I'm not naturally that competitive, but that sounds mad when you think about what I used to do for a job. In terms of sport, competition does bring the best out in me, but it can also turn me into someone I don't particularly like as well so I'd sooner lose and be a happy person than win and hate myself for being so aggressive – which hasn't always been the case.

The element of competition in *A League of Their Own*, Sky's sports-based comedy panel show, has taken on a life of its own. We have so many athletes who are either freshly retired, or on the cusp of retirement and that gamesmanship still exists. Jamie Redknapp loves to win and it might look like we're having a laugh, but it often becomes a proper battle. I shy away from it – even to the point where I'll throw the game sometimes. I won't really try. It gets a little bit embarrassing when you win all the challenges but things like that just come more naturally to me than the others. I think it's more of a case of the others not picking things – or in other words, being useless. We do all these sports that aren't particularly hard and I can turn my hand to stuff for some reason. That's the thing – I know so many people who can play so many sports better than me but for some reason I pick things up quickly, which is half the battle on *ALOTO*.

If I'm up against Romesh Ranganathan or Jamie, who's a fragile little soldier, I have to be careful not to damage them. Jamie can play a sport but he's delicate – we're always winding him up about it. Jack Whitehall, by his own admission, wouldn't be described as a rough-and-tumble type of lad. I'll end up doing something half-arsed, not to win, but purely because I find it uncomfortable listening to the praise and the over-the-top compliments for winning a silly task.

The only time I really tried on the show was with badminton. And this is a good example of what happens when my competitive side does come out. We did a badminton challenge and Jamie was clearly very confident with the shuttlecock (he was the area champion or something when he was down in Bournemouth as a kid). He's been egging it on, desperate to play badminton, so he could show off. I'd probably played once or twice, in the wind, in Morecambe, on a holiday or something. But I was watching it, thinking, *It can't be hard, it's a shuttlecock. It can't be that quick.*

So, I really started concentrating while Jamie was giving it the big one. I was just watching it, trying to figure the game out. We did a bit against the professional Olympians and I managed to return service, no problem. It was all about reactions and I knew I had it sussed. Then I watched Jamie play and I was studying him, watching him play like he was an opponent at cricket. I worked out how he hit it and from the serve where he was going. I could see how he stood and where he was vulnerable. *I've got you here!* I thought.

So, every serve, I hit it into the area where I knew he was weak. He couldn't get it. I could see him getting more and more frustrated. Usually in the challenges I'd be chatting but I didn't say a word. I ended up beating him and then rubbed it in his face. Afterwards, they set up a court for the rematch, but I refused to play. I said, 'No, I'm not playing this again. We've won.' It was maybe a bit over the top to let my competitive side loose on a TV badminton challenge, but on that occasion, beating Redknapp, it was definitely worth it!

Superheroes

I'd be a terrible superhero. I wouldn't want the pressure, it's too much responsibility. You'd be sat at home just getting settled and then someone would be screaming to go and get them. Then how do you decide who to help? I can't be in two places at once, I may as well not bother. Then you're all over the front pages for being a failed superhero and you can't have that. That's the whole celebrity thing. Some people think I've got some bizarre super power. It's just weird.

Other people I thought were heroes of the silver screen when I was growing up I'm not so sure about now. I've been watching the old James Bond movies recently, all the way through to the more recent Daniel Craig films. I watched *Casino Royale* and you believe Craig could do something in a fight. He looks capable, he looks quite hard, and the type of bloke a woman might fancy. I've realised I don't really like Bond but then I think sometimes I rebel against popular things for absolutely no reason. But here's the reason I had a rethink: it hit me when I was watching the movies from the seventies that this was a creepy old bloke who you'd warn your daughter about. I watched one, I think it was Roger Moore in *Octopussy*. He's on this bed with an aquarium in the background and there's this girl in her mid-twenties. He must be 50-odd, with his hairy back and he's just getting on to mount her. Giving a little wink to the camera on his way, like everyone was in on it and it's alright.

I was taken aback by how out-of-date it was and how I reacted to the scene. How can anybody defend that now? It wasn't on. Then he's fighting with someone who he's completely out of his depth with. Jaws would have ripped him apart, limb by limb – it's total nonsense.

To me, Daley Thompson, the decathlete, is probably the athlete who had the closest thing to the aura of a superhero. I remember watching him win his gold medals at the Los Angeles Olympics in 1984. Then afterwards we all ended up owning the 'Daley Thompson Decathlon' computer game for the Spectrum 48k, thundering away on rubber keys, cutting our hands to ribbons trying to make the little computer Daley win gold.

You can't help but admire what Daley achieved as an athlete. He has held world records in decathlon for decades, he's the ultimate Olympian. In an era where Britain were lucky to win a handful of medals, he was always a nailed-on winner. I've heard him speak about it at a black tie event – he was wearing a tracksuit for starters, which takes a bit of bottle. This is the guy who caused a massive stir for whistling the national anthem on the podium while collecting his gold at the Los Angeles Olympics in 1984. So he's the only person not wearing black tie. It made me laugh because he must be really special to get away with that. I've turned up at Lord's and had to borrow a tie to gain access to the Long Room, but he got in wearing his adidas shell suit to deliver his Q&A. They wouldn't have let crocodile hunter Steve Irwin in wearing shorts. The thing is, Daley did an event with running, throwing and jumping. It's the most accessible sport with no fancy kit required and he was the best in the world at it, completely dominating the sport.

Viv Richards was on a different level when I was growing up. He was such a talented cricketer and a huge personality. When I was 14, we went on a school trip to a Test match at Old Trafford. It was the only school trip we ever had and it was because one of my dad's mates sorted it out. He was also my games teacher and he wanted to go to the Test match, so we all went with him. So, there we were, watching Wasim Akram bowl and David Gower and Graham Gooch batting. Less than two years later, I was sat in a dressing room with Wasim. I was still a kid and now going into a room with all these players I sort of thought of as superheroes – well, I just lost the power of speech around them.

It was bonkers but during the World Cup in 1999, all the teams were there for the opening ceremony in the hotel and I was at the bar with Wasim, having a chat. Just then, Viv comes strolling into town; he's got his swagger and everyone just steps aside as he comes through. He comes straight up to Wasim, high fives him and then puts his hand up for me. I was blown away, thinking, *Oh, this is for me, isn't it?*

Then he started talking to me about my batting and I was just trying to process the fact that one of the greats was talking about me playing cricket. It was the weirdest thing. I had the same feeling chatting with John Barnes and Mike Tyson – you're trying to have a conversation and ignore the voice in your head screaming, 'IT'S IRON MIKE!!'

As for John Barnes, he was a bit of a hero in our house growing up. When he scored that amazing solo effort for England v Brazil – that was pure magic. My brother's a Liverpool fan and I was for a bit because they won everything in the eighties. My first kit was the Crown Paints one in the late eighties – it was a birthday present off my mum, dad and my brother. And of course, John really stood up to the vile racism in the sport at the time, which must have taken a lot of courage.

Barnesy came on *ALOTO* and I was playing it cool, like I used to do with Jamie when we first started working together. Then I got on a train from London on my way back to Manchester and I saw John walking past the carriage. I was sat there in the first coach where they have the kitchen and I could see him outside. I knew him now and so any normal reaction would be to knock on the window and say, 'Hi, John!' But I couldn't because I was thinking, *That's John Barnes! He doesn't want to sit with me. Why would he want to sit with me?* I thought I'd missed my chance as he disappeared for a bit but then I saw him approaching and not being able to find a seat.

He opened the carriage door and spotted me and I was thinking, *John Barnes looks happy to see me here!* He sat down and I just talked to him all the way home for two and a half hours. He was telling me about when he came over from Jamaica, how he got spotted for Watford and how he loves watching cricket with his family. He told me about his kids and what he's doing and how he's got this big lump on his shoulder where he dislocated it. I couldn't get over that I was sat there talking to John Barnes. I'm not even a massive football fan – but it's JOHN BARNES!

I've always thought footballers get a bad rap. Though, no pun intended with Barnsey's efforts in New Order's 'World in Motion'. Let's be honest, they're generally not the most articulate when it comes to their interviews but they want to be footballers. You wouldn't put a chat show host on a pitch and critique his football skills, it's not what they're there for.

People have preconceptions about players and what they see in a minute and a half, two-minute interview after a game. One, they've been running around for 90 minutes. Two, you've no idea what's going on in their lives off the pitch. If they've just lost, and the interviewer is going to drop a shit sandwich on them, you can't be surprised why they're giving you nothing. Yet we're hypercritical of their delivery and responses.

If I went back to have my career again I would have handled the post-match interviews completely differently. I don't think I'd have done any of them unless I absolutely had to. I tried it all different ways. I was nice to reporters, I one-worded them. You couldn't win. I wish I'd have been a bit more honest. I think that's what sport's lacking now a little bit. The problem is that you never feel like you can give an honest answer in a press conference if you'll just get hammered for it. So, you'd go in, you'd have your press liaison next to you, you'd get a briefing about what the journalists are going to ask you or the angle they're going to go down. You're then told, 'This is what we want you to say, this is where you lead it.'

CONFIDENCE

I think Swedish striker Zlatan Ibrahimović is brilliant. He's a guilty pleasure of mine, him. I'd have been a bit more Zlatan if I had my time again. I'd have loved to have thought I could be in a position where I could front up that level of self-belief and confidence. There is a great press conference quote from him where he is asked if he is arrogant. He replies: 'I'm not arrogant, I'm confident.'

Let's be honest, he's not Cristiano Ronaldo or Lionel Messi. He's almost created this persona which has made him a better footballer, and people fear him and I love that. When he says, 'You don't compare men to lions,' and 'I've never been a boy, I've always been a man,' all of that stuff is pure theatre.

I felt like I was often covering up my insecurities when a microphone was in front of me. We can all be a bit more Zlatan, I think.

CHAPTER THREE

WORK

*'I was going to get this job by being myself or
I was going to lose this job by being myself.'*

Preston Woolies

Other than playing cricket, my first real job was working behind the record counter at Woolworths in Preston. My brother Chris was working at Woolies while he was at university to earn some extra cash, so I got a job beside him and I absolutely loved it. Though I'd started getting paid to play cricket, you didn't get paid in the winter, so I had to rely on my job at Woolworths.

I should probably explain for some of the younger readers what Woolworths is. Come to think of it, in the era of streaming and TikTok, maybe I should explain what a record is too. Anyway, if you've ever heard of a pick'n'mix, you've got Woolies to thank for it.

If I tell anyone born before 1985 I worked in Woolies, they automatically assume I must have stolen from the pick'n'mix. Of course, they are completely correct – I did. They were long shifts and I needed the sugar to get me through. But chocolate mice, bon bons and Black Jacks were the least of their worries. I may also have been involved in acquiring a PlayStation.

You see, I found out about a very helpful technical term early on in my career in the retail industry called 'shrinkage'. I think it was designed to take care of damaged goods or faulty items that were returned to the store after purchase. A percentage, if you like, that was written into the P&L to account for stuff going wrong. You could also describe it as a perk for the likes of me and my big brother, Chris.

So, here's what used to happen, and it was an experience that shaped me as a young man. I've squared off what you're about to read as Robin Hood-style heroics, looking after the poorer families of the North-West. Customers would come in who I happened to know and it just so happened the items they were selecting somehow didn't go through the till accurately. In fact, they didn't go through at all. It was Christmas time after all and the people I was looking out for couldn't afford a PlayStation, so in my mind, I was doing a good deed and I stand by it to this day. That said, when Woolworths went under, it did occur to me that the scale of the light fingers multiplied across their stores nationwide would probably have played a significant part.

Back in the early nineties, there were no infrared handguns to clock the items as they were going through. Nope, I'm afraid to inform you all those items just mysteriously disappeared through my good pal 'shrinkage'. That wasn't all, I'd often give customers some change for the bus fare home, too, like a lanky Jim Bowen from *Bullseye*. Again, for younger readers, look it up on YouTube. The shrinkage situation was a classic contradiction in terms. If anything, while I was working there, it was getting bigger. It started escalating to an extent where I had to draw a line. I do feel really bad, and I've talked about it on TV. I knew it was time to stop when a guy I didn't know came up to me, winked at me and asked for a PlayStation. He had no means to pay for it.

Security back then was down to the least fearful human beings plucked from the dole queue to work as store detectives. Normally it was lads who couldn't run the length of themselves just strolling around, not even worthy of the word 'milling' around, thinking about what they were going to order from Greggs for brekkie, lunch or dinner.

I can't claim to have been any good at my work. In the last week of October and the first week of November, I was tasked with hanging all the Christmas decorations. It still wasn't done on Christmas Eve! I used to sit at the top of this big ladder and listen to Elvis's *Essential Collection*, when they let me put it on. All the usual Christmas music was on loop – Paul McCartney's 'Wonderful Christmastime', Slade's 'Merry Christmas Everybody' and that Song by Wizzard, 'I Wish It

Could Be Christmas Everyday'. I'd just sit there and watch the world go by with those songs on loop.

Not only was I responsible for a few items going missing, I didn't really contribute much to preventing others being lifted. The technology to catch shoplifters with detectors at the door was still a long way off. There would be a series of bells that would go off, activated by staff, if a shoplifter made a run for it. It was one of my jobs to make the chase after them, mainly because the store detectives were concentrating on being deterrents rather than a crack response unit. I was fast back then and I can recall one occasion when the bells went off and I vaulted the desk and went after a shoplifter – running past the girls on the Pick'n'Mix, giving it the big 'un – down the street and hanging a right to Winckley Square. Then this lad just turned around and squared up to me and said, 'Right, come on then!' I completely bottled it. He had a pack of TDK 90 tapes and I thought, *Nah, you're alright, mate. I'm not getting my head kicked in for a packet of cassettes.*

Actually, now I think about it, I was indirectly responsible for quite a bit of damage to Preston's retail industry. When I was doing work experience with school, I told my guidance teacher I wanted to be a professional sportsman. You've heard it a million times before and I was no different with the 'Oh, yeah? No chance' reply.

My aspirations were matched up with a stint of work experience at Champion Sport, in Debenhams. I had to do a week and write a report about it. I had plenty to talk about because we got robbed while I was there – and not by me. Initially, anyway.

My boss at Debenhams said, 'I'm just going to nip upstairs for five minutes. Can you stand around a bit and keep an eye on things?'

I replied, 'Yeah. Of course, I've got this.' What he didn't legislate for was the appearance of some attractive girls around my age, maybe a bit older. These girls came in and started talking to me and I very awkwardly spoke back.

What I didn't know was that they were a decoy while we were getting robbed by their accomplices. When the boss came back down to the storeroom with all the trainers, we realised loads had gone missing. It's fair to say I got in serious trouble for that, even though it wasn't really my fault.

* * *

Somehow my brother Chris reached a level of seniority at Woolies that he was store manager on the night shift from time to time. One of Preston's infamous nightclubs, Tokyo Joe's, was a few doors down the street, so if he was on duty through the night, we used to go in to Woolies after a big session. It was brilliant – eating all the sweets, a few more drinks to sober up and we'd just sit there having a laugh.

The nostalgia makes me smile just thinking about it

because it was so funny. There was one occasion I remember, where my brother was on nights and he accidentally locked one of his colleagues in the shop overnight. It was his responsibility to make sure the store was cleared, everything was in order for the next day and firmly closed for the rest of the night but somehow, he managed to lock the poor girl inside. It's funny but it's not. She thought if she moved all the alarms would go off and she'd be in massive trouble so, from late that evening until eight o'clock in the morning, she just sat still, terrified. Apparently, the next morning, she was traumatised.

People have forgotten about Woolies, which makes me sad. It seemed like one of those constants on the High Street, but one by one, they are all disappearing – BHS, Debenhams, Woolies. That's such a shame because it was such a great life experience for me and my brother and I can imagine how important those shops have been over the years, giving other people their first jobs or a proper career.

When I was at Woolies I was paid £3.77 an hour as a full-time member of staff. I'd get on my bike from my house and pedal into Preston. Having a proper job when you are a teenager is really important, I think. It helped me grow up, taught me a lot about the real world. It also taught me what I didn't want to be in my life – disrespectful and rude to folk working in retail jobs. Some people would come in and see a young lad like me working there and look down on him. This might sound like a cliché from the eighties and nineties, but it gave me a dislike of students. A number of them, not all of them of course, would be really condescending and rude.

A couple of my mates ended up marrying the girls I worked with. Everyone knows everyone in Preston, it can be a bit incestuous. There was a great fella called John who got me a pair of knock-off Oakley sunglasses that I wore for cricket. Everyone I worked with was a bit older and I felt like every day had some small life lesson.

Find Your Bumble

One of the most important life lessons I've learned is to surround yourself with people you can learn from. Characters you admire, who you want to make proud. As a young cricketer, I was lucky enough to have people like Bumble (David Lloyd) and Mike Summerbee, the Manchester City legend, as mentors – people I really looked up to and listened to.

I was working at Trent Bridge recently and I had a flashback to something amazing that meant the world to me in my cricket career, and it was a good reminder of how to conduct yourself in professional sport. Two nights before my Test debut for England, Michael Atherton, Angus Fraser and a cricket writer, Michael Henderson, took me out for dinner. Michael Henderson got stuck into people with a bit of humour and he had a big reputation, so it was important they brought him along to introduce me.

He was like nobody I had ever met in my life before. He was posh and had opinions on everything, he was quite forthright and when I met him, he had upset so many people in his articles. I found him quite funny and I got the feeling he wrote his stuff for his own amusement, which I liked even more. We went to this beautiful restaurant, Harts, and had some amazing wine. That was a really nice touch, it was a big deal for me. Bumble and Mike Summerbee had the same touch of class about the way they looked out for me.

I met Mike at a function when I was 17; we had a mutual friend who introduced us. We would go on holidays together because I always enjoyed being around him, hearing his stories. I've always liked older company – it must come from being in dressing rooms with older players from such a young age with my dad.

Bumble, who I have spoken about a hell of a lot, was such a significant character in my development and not just as a cricketer, but as a man as well. Obviously my family played a huge part in supporting me too, but Bumble was the one who helped me because I needed someone to back me. I didn't need someone to teach me how to hit a ball, it was about affirmation and getting that confidence from someone who could put an arm around me. He backed me to the hilt and he loved me. I felt that and it gave me huge confidence. I'm just grateful I had people like him in my life as a young professional sportsman. I remember him saying 'Don't do anything that doesn't make your mother proud,' but I broke that rule a few times over the years. He always backed me more than I backed myself, he believed in me more than I believed in myself and that started to rub off on me.

Bumble was incredibly kind to me. He insisted that I be allowed to field in the slips, a position usually reserved for the old pros – 'He's brilliant, this lad, you'll see, never drops them, he can catch pigeons.' He really lifted my spirits, but then in the first over from Wasim Akram, I dropped a catch. Then I put two more down, at which point Wasim is going crazy and he says, 'Get that boy out of the slips or I'll throw him a fucking pigeon myself!'

The consistency of his trust in me, it made me thrive. He had such a reassuring manner, I kept thinking, *If he believes in me so much, why can't I back myself?*

It's probably the most significant lesson I could pass on to any parent or coach. If you can play the David Lloyd role in a young person's life – give them confidence, encourage them even in the smallest things – then you absolutely should. It goes such a long way. Having somebody believe in you is the springboard for everything in life.

* * *

When I started in the second team at Lancashire, you used to knock on the door to get in the first team dressing room – you could just walk right in the second team dressing room. When I started, you still had to tidy up or clear away whatever you were told to sort out. If you look at the All Blacks in Rugby Union, the healthy, respectful culture around their dressing room is something else. The captain chooses where you sit and welcomes you in and introduces you – that's a mark of true class. I love it that wearing the national jersey, of one of the most famous international teams, doesn't preclude you from tidying the dressing room after a game. The All Blacks always leave a dressing room as they find it – immaculate. And why shouldn't they? That's something every dressing room should learn from.

Just before my time in the game, the senior players would treat the younger ones like shit and there's still a bit of a hangover from that time. What that experience did for me was important because I knew I would do things differently when I was a senior player.

As an older player, I always championed the younger kids so within the dressing room it was clear no bullying would go on. Later on, I liked being around the younger lads. I loved the naïvety of it, I loved watching them come through.

When I entered the dressing room for the first time with England, I walked in with my kit, well aware that everyone changes in the same spot at every ground you would visit. I assumed someone would move up for me. Nothing doing. So, I went in the back room with the washing machines and changed in there for my first ever game for England.

This is a bit fucking weird, this. This isn't right, I thought.

After that experience, whenever a young player came into the dressing room, I'd go completely the other way. Ultimately, this new player is in my team and I want to win. I want this lad thinking he's the best he can be. I don't want him worried because he feels unwelcome. I just never got that attitude – it was rotten. It's the same for me in telly – the runners are there to help you, to make you better, to make the show better – so that starts from the person at the bottom all the way up to the top.

Packing It In

My career was plagued with injuries. I had a chronic back problem from the age of 13 to about 22. Then in 2004 I had my first ankle operation. This led to six or seven more, as the problem wasn't fixed. I was surviving on painkilling injections in the 2005 Ashes. The ankle problems led to knee problems. In 2009 ahead of the start of The Ashes, I had a routine cartilage repair on my right knee. Routine, that was, unless the doctor found any bone damage. The good news was that that was a one in 1 in 10,000. When I woke up and saw his face, I instantly knew I was that 1 in 10,000. The doctor sorted out the cartilage but he didn't want to touch the bone damage until he'd spoken to me as it involved a serious procedure called a microfracture, where they fracture your knee to regenerate the bone. That kind of surgery would have meant months out of cricket, and not being able to play in The Ashes in 2009. I was bizarrely grateful that he hadn't operated as it allowed me to play, even though I knew the damage I was doing to myself meant there was a good chance it would be the end of my career.

I played in the first Test of The Ashes in Cardiff and managed to bowl well over 90mph. But I needed the jabs to keep the pain away as it was becoming nearly too much to handle. Monty Panesar and Jimmy Anderson got us out of jail with some magnificent batting. After the game I headed to London because I had a hastily arranged medical appointment the next morning. I needed something to help with the pain. I needed to speak to my doctor, although I knew there was nothing to be done other than surgery, which would have meant the end of my series. I popped down to the bar for an innocent drink, thought I'd have a couple of pints and settle down for the night, but it didn't quite work out like that.

So, I had gone downstairs for a few pints in The Landmark and Oasis were there and those Leicester lads in the rock band Kasabian showed up. We drank right through the night. Serge

Pizzorno and Tom Meighan had played a big show and a load of their mates had been out at the gig. The after-show party rumbled into the hotel in the wee small hours before they all went back to Leicester the next day.

The night was certainly a wild one – like something you would imagine in the early seventies with the Rolling Stones. Everyone was hammered, staff were trying to calm it down, guests were complaining.

Looking back, I think part of me was celebrating a great Test match and part of me wanted to forget about my knee and let off a bit of steam.

The next morning, I left at 8am to see my knee specialist and I was in a world of trouble. I stank of booze. I'd been on whisky, shots, lager, wine – everything going. Luckily, Andy Williams, the specialist, was a good lad. I think some operations were done on my ankle just because the surgeons could, but Andy was different. He always said, 'My dad's a builder. I do the same job, but with different tools.' He's from Bristol and it was always reassuring to hear how direct he was. He's a great fella.

I said, 'Mate, I stink, I went to bed at 6am.'

He was fine until I told him my knee was totally knackered.

'Yeah, I know,' he said. 'It's probably a good thing you are half-pissed because you've got a decision to make.' He broke the news in a really direct way, but I needed to know: 'You're not fit to play, I need to operate and it's touch and go. If I do it, it's not guaranteed it's going to work.' He said if I played the next few games it could end my career early and the knee couldn't be repaired.

I remember being in Carluccio's across the road in Marylebone after the appointment. I had five double espressos just trying to get my head straight with what was happening. What was I doing? I was hammered and my career was ending.

I decided to retire from Test cricket after that series. I planned to announce it because I just wanted the weight off my shoulders but when I went to tell the coach Andy Flower, he wasn't having it.

He told me straight, 'Nah. I don't want you to do that. It'll take all the focus away from the team.'

I thought that would be a good thing, because I was more than happy to take the pressure on my shoulders. I was more than happy to handle that, because my motive was to help the team in any way I could. If I became the story, it meant they could get on with things and concentrate on playing.

Throughout the next Test match my condition was deteriorating. I was having to take more and more painkillers and receive more and more injections during the match to control the pain. Getting up on the final morning I was in a world of trouble. We still needed to take five wickets, but I couldn't even dress myself. My body was shutting down. Rachael put my clothes on for me and took me to the ground. I was using cortisone like Popeye uses spinach. But I think the effects of Popeye's spinach last a bit longer. It turned out to be a day to remember. I got five wickets and it was England's first Ashes win at Lord's since 1934.

We went on to finish the summer of 2009 on a high, beating Australia 2–1 at The Oval, and I managed to run out Aussie captain Ricky Ponting – a great way to bow out. But I had played through a lot of pain. My knee was in bits. I had needed to exorcise the demons of what had happened in the previous series, when we were hammered 5–0 by the Aussies. I had to play – there was no decision to make. My body was at breaking point, but I wouldn't swap that decision. I retired from Test cricket at the end of the series. By then I could barely move. Playing in that series possibly cost me three years of my career.

As the team celebrated into the early hours, I was nil by mouth at midnight. I wanted to have the operation that I'd delayed months before as soon as I could. It was too late. I would never regain my fitness afterwards. I never played for England again.

The following year, I knew it was over. I was in The Malmaison Glasgow having breakfast with Andy Williams and my physio Dave when it was decided it was time to do something else. Cricket was no longer an option. It's mad,

I was exactly the same age as Jamie Redknapp when he chucked it and both of us done in by our knees in the end. As much as I like Andy, I was hoping I would never see him again in a professional capacity, but unfortunately in 2011, he had to get his tools out once more to perform an operation called an Osteotomy that was worse than all the others put together, just so I could walk relatively pain free. This entailed breaking my leg and straightening it, taking part of my hip out and packing it into my knee, and then holding it together with a metal clamp, which is nailed down on to my shin. This was to try to prevent the need for a plastic knee replacement for as long as possible.

Following the operation they put me on self-administered morphine. I was out of it. Darren Gough came to see me, but afterwards I couldn't remember if I'd dreamed it or not. No one would believe me that he'd been there. It took six months before I got him to verify it.

Starting Over

The cold hard fact is that I only ever wanted to be a cricketer. That was everything for me. And when my career finished, it felt like everything was gone. At 31, I felt like I was 16 again – trying to rebuild a career and stumbling onto the next thing is as unsettling as it gets.

I needed to get away from cricket for a period of time,

that was evident, because it was just eating me up inside not being able to play. Maybe I could have gone into commentary but at that moment, the thought of sitting there and talking about the game that I was no longer involved in was spirit crushing. Moving away was the best thing I could do – the physical distance from the game and the people and the memories was so important for my head. Now though that's slightly different – I'm 43, I shouldn't be playing cricket, I'm too old.

Anyway, when my playing career ended, I must admit, my door wasn't being knocked down by people offering me exciting jobs in cricket broadcasting. I'd done a bit for Sky in the past and there was a sprinkling of enquiries when I was a bit younger. I'm not sure if they were that bothered, really, because I'd said a few things about them and I'd also said a few things about some of the people who worked for them. I didn't hold back so perhaps I blotted my copybook a little bit.

Everyone thinks because you're a cricket player that you can just go in and commentate, but the game has moved on a lot when it comes to commentary. A lot of the older players were rumbled because guys like Rob Key came in, Nasser Hussain, Mike Atherton. Of the old guard, Bumble raised the game massively.

You see it with football and Gary Neville, much as it pains me to give him a compliment, it's his job and he treats it like he's a professional in a new arena with the same effort and application he put in as a player at Manchester United. He still winds me up, though. I've known his family for years and Gary has always been the same – he's busy! The analysis and punditry are at such a high level, they really break it down for you with remarkable technology. It's not just turning up and telling a few stories and saying how much you drank last night, with the odd 'Back in my day . . .' Commentary has moved on and you've got to know the game inside out. The viewers consume so much of it, it's like a university module running 48 weeks of the year, training armchair supporters up as experts. That's partly why I didn't leap into it straight away, as well as because I didn't want to sit watching something I thought I should still be playing – it would have been too painful.

* * *

I didn't want the lifestyle of a cricketer without having the joy of playing and so coaching just wasn't an option either. It wasn't for me because it was far too raw not playing but also I don't think I'd have got a job for love nor money because the perception of me in the sport wasn't great. I think the boozing was probably a big turn-off and I'd been outspoken about so many people in powerful positions.

I've got my first two coaching qualifications but the first

level you can pass for explaining how to hold a bat at the right end. You get onto Level 2 if you can identify a cricket ball. Passing Level 2 is a bit harder but it's all based on coaching at a level with kids and organising nets and structure. Level 3 starts getting a bit more interesting and Level 4 is like a university degree.

I was really taken aback by Arsène Wenger when we met on *The Graham Norton Show*. He was so smart and knowledgeable. He talked about football being an art, but how much science was also involved. A coach's job at the top level is making the players feel the best they can when they walk out onto the field. Within cricket, it's upside down: the coaching should be done when the players are younger, the Barcelona model. I would love to do Lancashire and England but the real work is done with kids, which is something I would sooner do. You can shape players, but it's neglected in cricket because you get paid more at the higher level. Me, I'm more interested in academy and younger cricketers.

Cricket had to become more professional, and now it's played by athletes.

When I started, there was a huge drinking culture. You got pissed and that was the end of it. Throughout my career, it started changing and by the back end of my playing days, my body shape was changing for the better. Somehow, I was getting much fitter despite the injuries.

There was no fitness or pre-season when I started. You would turn up in nets twice a week for a month before the season began. At Lancashire, from 2003 onwards it became more professional. I really bought into it. OK, I would have a bacon butty at Lord's and steak for lunch, but I was fitter than anyone towards the end. If you watch how much I played, in the different countries and the heat and humidity, that's when I enjoyed it. And that was all down to hard work and training with our physio, Dave Rooster Roberts, or on my own.

I practically lived with the physio for the last six years of my career. He came with me as a package and always travelled with me. Not everyone knew, I wanted to keep some mystery about my life – I didn't want people to think I was working as hard as I was behind the scenes. The lads and others just thought I was driven and committed, but I was actually really fit. The shape of me, I didn't look fit because I didn't have abs. That's how I got the Jacamo menswear deal – because I'm not a normal shape. When I got to a normal shape, that's when they got rid of me! I wasn't built like conventional athletes.

When I finished my career, I genuinely thought I had missed out on the best years. At 31, my batting was struggling but getting better, my bowling had never been as fast – I had it on tap. So when I look back, from 31, I had three years I could have had at my best. I always play down my career and say I'm not as good as others but I am confident that nobody could have done what I did. I was battling depression, bulimic and always injured. Who else could have achieved what I did with three serious issues stacked against them?

I was either hangry – angry because I was hungry – or sometimes hungover. For years I have played it down, but I now have a sense of pride about overcoming those obstacles.

I've been quite humble because my Test statistics don't stack up. The first quarter of my career, I couldn't bowl and I don't think I could bat. The last third, I was so much better. Against the very best opposition, I was always in it. I wasn't always up for it against some of the smaller teams and that's where you can make stats sing.

When you look at numbers and big name players, they can be misleading. I only care about the stats when we pulled something out the bag or we won against the best. So many stats are pulled out from dead games. I take pride in the number of games I influenced.

I read an article the other day about The Hundred. It was written around Ben Stokes and the mental health issues he faces, playing on the field in the midst of it. It brought it all home for me.

Depression is a numbness. It's anxiety I had all the way through my career in cricket. I wouldn't want to take a break like Ben. For me, I knew it would only get worse if I didn't play. If I walked away, it would have sent me further down. In fact, it would have been dangerous for me to do that.

It's hard to offer advice – people have their own theories and take advice from experts – I can only speak from my own experience. I distanced myself and became quite insular. Cricket was so important because it could change or alter how I was feeling. It didn't always work, but it was a safe place to give me the chance to change my mood. Retiring at 31, not having cricket there, I found other ways to escape – usually drink, but I managed to get a good hold of that.

A League of Their Own: Courage and Conviction

I'd be lying if I said that a lot of work I have done since cricket hasn't been transactional. I have done jobs that have been solely for the money, to get somewhere or to push further. But that's real life – sometimes you have to pay the bills. The last year has been such a big reminder of that. Being able to support your family, regardless of what you do, is justification for doing it.

In 2013, I appeared with The Muppets on telly when I was half-cut after a massive night out. I'm sat there talking to a fucking puppet, thinking, *Jesus Christ! What am I doing here?* There are other jobs I have taken when I've tried to get myself in good favour for something else or get where I wanted to go – *A League of Their Own* used to be like that for me.

WORK

My agent in late 2009 was Chubby Chandler. He told me that I had received a request to go on the pilot of an ambitious new panel show which they were aiming to make into a flagship show on Sky One. They were keen to get me involved as a team captain and said it was being hosted by James Corden but I had no idea who he was. Chubby told me that the stand-up comedian John Bishop was on it, but I didn't have a clue who he was either. I had seen the presenter Georgie Thompson on the news, so I had some idea about her and Jamie Redknapp had signed up by then, though I had only met him once at that point.

I immediately said I didn't fancy it, even though the money was alright. At the time I was injured, my knee and ankle were on the cusp of giving up, and all I was interested in was getting back to playing again, so it went away. Not long after that, I retired from cricket and the show reared its head again. Former Twenty20 international captain Stuart Broad had filmed the pilot, which I watched. No disrespect to Stuart, but I knew straight away I could deliver better than he did.

At that point I was still saying no to the approaches, then I moved agents to Richard Thompson, a week before the show was going to be filmed. Neil Morrissey, from *Men Behaving Badly* and the first few series of *Line of Duty*, was the blue team captain. Thommo said to me, 'Are you sure you don't want to do this?' I'm very grateful to him for his perseverance; he talked me into doing it and poor Neil got bumped off the show, but there you go. That's how it works in TV. He got *Death in Paradise* in the end, so it wasn't like he was going hungry.

So, I got on there and I absolutely hated it, I really did. I was sat there ten days in and it was an effort just to get through it. I felt like that little lad again who was going into the dressing room and I wasn't really sure how to speak, what to do, how to interact with people properly. I was sat there feeling so conspicuous and I'm sure Jamie must have been feeling the same – we would glance across the studio at each other in panic. James Corden was finding his way as well, Bish was as good as gold, Georgie Thompson was lovely and we got on really well, but I hated the first four or five series. I was honestly going to walk, it just wasn't right for me, but I love doing the show now.

You look at everyone who has been on that programme and it really propelled us all to another level. James was on the cusp of really making it and he would say it gave him the confidence to go on to the next level. Jamie now is chalk and cheese to what he was when he started; I was the same. We would come off and be told we were great but I felt I hadn't said anything. I would tell them that and they would reply, 'Well, what you did do was great!' It was weird getting used

WORK

to that. I felt like it was a bit of fluff. I came from dressing room culture and was ready for some fierce criticism of my performance. TV is too subjective for me and that's the bit that I find hard to get my head around sometimes. There can be no rhyme and reason to the appraisal of your performance.

There was an executive at Sky called Stuart Murphy who really helped me out more than anyone. He would tell me things straight, how I wanted to hear them. I had dinner with him once and he explained how I was on the show and he called it right, he was spot on. He gave me the kind of direction I needed so I could correct what I was doing wrong, do something about it and improve. I loved that, it was the development and coaching I needed. Not too much affirmation but enough to make sure I didn't lose my bottle. He pointed out that I looked like I wasn't interested a lot of the time and he was right; he told me to get more involved and be assertive. He said he found me funny when I was reacting to things, so I should back myself and have conviction – as if I was delivering some sledging on the field or dishing out some stick in the dressing room.

I think the sporting side has really helped in my development on TV. For one, you don't mind brutal honesty. That's so important – you have to learn to take constructive criticism and sometimes deal with criticism that comes without any foundation. When I was still playing, the times I thought

I was cracking it, almost every time, that's when it went wrong. I won't do that again with TV. And as a life lesson, it's worth remembering complacency really trips you up if it goes unchallenged.

When Bish left, I phoned up CPL, the production company who make the show, and asked if I could have Jack Whitehall. They thought it was a bit leftfield but they listened and made the move for Jack. It was perfect timing and it worked a treat. And now I can claim credit for Jack Whitehall's career – the little melt.

You look back at some of the opportunities we've had. They are ridiculous. We were dressed up as cheerleaders for the first game the LA Rams played in Los Angeles for years in front of 90,000. Jack tried to engage the players in conversation and he was told to fuck right off! They were not having him at all.

If *ALOTO* was going on air for the first time right now, I don't think we would survive. It would be cancelled before the end of the series. It was poor to start with and needed time to evolve and for all of us to find our way. It took me a while to really find my stride and without that time, we wouldn't be doing the jobs we all have now.

In that first series we had comedian Jimmy Carr sticking his head in a bucket of water to see how long he can hold his breath. Now we're bringing in full swimming pools, we're abseiling from towers and Jamie's breaking world records (while breaking his wrist. He's such an eggshell, that boy!).

The Andros Townsend Moment

I watched some footage of Sean Connery just after he passed away from when he was on Michael Parkinson's chat show. He made a comment about what we would probably call 'styling it out'. In his Scottish brogue, he was saying that you have to be fully prepared to make a fool of yourself if you have any hope of making it as an actor. He also used the most powerful swear word in the dictionary but I've chosen to keep this polite.

A League of Their Own helped me with the Sean Connery philosophy. I remember on the first series, me and Jamie Redknapp were always saying we wouldn't do the games they had dreamt up because we didn't want to commit to making complete idiots of ourselves. Or if we did do them, we would often do them half-arsed – and it would come across so badly on TV because you weren't committed.

If I had to give you an example of someone we can all learn from when it comes to getting in the spirit of things, one athlete stands out. His name has become synonymous for all of us on *ALOTO* with the right attitude to adopt to anything you're confronted with. It was such an eye-opening moment,

I feel like I should be giving this man a mention in the introduction to this book.

The man in question is Everton midfielder Andros Townsend. Bask in his name; he is an absolute game changer and we owe a lot to him for what he did when he came on *ALOTO* in 2014. I knew at the time he was an England prospect and he was playing for Spurs in the Premier League and in Europe. That was about it. I never normally get excited about footballers coming on the show unless it was someone like AC Milan and Holland legend Ruud Gullit. Andros has changed that. I can't wait to find out on every show if we're about to uncover another secret Andros Townsend.

So, Andros is there and he's told he has to dress up as a space hopper and bounce on a treadmill while singing 'Stand By Me'. We all doubted that he would do it. In fact, none of us thought he'd agree.

We couldn't have got it more wrong: he absolutely smashed it. He could sing a bit and he was utterly committed to the job in hand in such an impressive way.

We call it 'The Andros Townsend Moment' and everyone on the show is measured against it now, including us. I'll often say, 'If Andros can do it, I can do it.' If you haven't seen it, get on YouTube and it will improve your day.

There is always stuff Jamie doesn't want to do on the show. Don't get me wrong, I don't want to do a lot of the ideas they have, but when I see that Jamie doesn't want to do them, I want to do them even more. That may sound like a contradiction, but when I know Jamie is not enjoying something that much, I actually really do then. When people come up to me and say, 'That must have been amazing when . . .' it's genuinely just work to me, but because we have access to all these amazing things, it becomes the norm, which is weird. It's a ridiculous situation when you think about it.

Every time I do something big on the show, like singing Elvis' 'Suspicious Minds' in the full seventies Vegas jumpsuit, wig, aviators and sideburns, I always think I've bitten off more than I can chew. If you don't watch it, the show will often end with a big set piece. Jamie has done 'Rapper's Delight' by The Sugarhill Gang with John Barnes and I often get myself into these positions where I don't truly believe I can do whatever I've been challenged to and I don't know what's going to happen or how it will work out, but it makes you feel alive.

It was the same with cricket in a way. And I battled through those nerves and every time I emerged a bit stronger, a bit braver and added a slither of extra confidence. As that process happened, I learned to enjoy the feeling.

It's something you have to embrace to improve and excel: the feeling of being uncomfortable. I truly believe it's in those moments you start to improve, develop and learn. I was working with Jason Fox, one of the Drill Sergeants on *SAS:*

Who Dares Wins, on the latest episode of *ALOTO Road Trip* and he said, 'Learn to be comfortable being uncomfortable.' It's where development happens, sports coaches will tell you that – when you are outside your comfort zone, you improve.

I'm under no illusions there are some great TV presenters out there and I don't class myself among them. There are people who have worked in TV for years, who have trained to do it, and telly is all they've ever wanted to do and I know they're saying, 'Why the fuck is that cricketer presenting *Top Gear*?' The one thing I try and do, and what I feel my true strength on television is, is when I react to stuff happening around me.

With *ALOTO*, I work with Clyde Holcroft and Fraser Steele. The best material we come up with is when me, Clyde and Fraser are chatting in the dressing room. They choose the topics and we just have a laugh about it and that's where we find the laughs. It's there in front of me because we have worked together to get all the material we have laughed about in our preparation. But if I ever just rely on it, I know I've had a bad show. If I turn to notes or something prepared, I feel like I haven't been spontaneous enough or my reaction to things hasn't been right. Forgetting everything else and instead, attempting to be in the moment as much as possible is key to the best results.

I genuinely believe that's another lesson in life: you have to try to live as much as you can in the moment. It's not helpful to punish yourself over things that haven't gone well in the immediate past, or spend too much time worrying about what lies ahead. Being in that moment is where the sweet spot lies.

King of the Jungle

I went to Australia at Christmas 2014, Rachael and the kids came out with me as I'd signed for Brisbane Heat to play in the T20 Big Bash League but I just wasn't good enough anymore. I'd been retired for a few years and I'd played a couple of games for Lancashire, which had gone alright and that turned a few heads. I found myself getting offered a contract, which was probably a nostalgia signing, looking back. I was obviously asked about my knee because I'd been told I'd never run again by a doctor, back in 2010. I knew there were a lot of things I couldn't do, but I convinced myself I'd be all right.

The deal included some broadcasting commitments, including commentary, and there was also a show called *The Project* that I was going to co-host on Tuesdays and Thursdays. It was a current affairs show, similar in style to the BBC's *The One Show*, but parts of it could be quite highbrow on occasion. That said, other parts could be full Alan Partridge. One minute, you'd be talking to an MP down the line about the Australian budget forecast and the next, you'd be going to a break with a squirrel on a skateboard.

Looking back, I have to laugh at some of the stuff I found myself doing. One night, I sang James Blunt's 'You're Beautiful' as we were going into a break. I still don't know how that happened but I think it was because they left the sound on in rehearsals and I was messing about. The director must have heard it and next thing I'm being cued up to sing by my co-host, Waleed Aly, who I suspect was enjoying trying to chuck me under a bus. It didn't work though, oh no! I was in my element and delivered a great performance.

There's a lesson in TV right there – remember when you're mic'd up! I was a bit of a novelty on the programme but I made it my mission to start surprising them with good research and asking proper questions, as well as all the other rubbish.

When that job on *The Project* came in, I was there for three months, working two or three nights a week. It was a great experience and it gave me an insight into presenting on live TV, which stood me well for the future.

* * *

Having Australia in my life has been a weird one. Beating them at cricket has opened up the Aussie market massively. They took to me and I think it's common for anyone who does really well against them, they seem to take to that. I want to be really clear, though: I'm not one of them! I'm from Preston, but I'm pleased they like me.

I've had this relationship with Australia which has been life-changing; from 2005 and The Ashes, it has been amazing. I've got a lot of gratitude towards Australia and the people, it's something I never expected.

I was in the Australian version of *I'm A Celebrity . . . Get Me Out Of Here!* in 2015, which I'm duty-bound to remind everyone I won. I was last one out – I was King of the Jungle!

The story behind the jungle is mad. I wasn't in from the start but after a week and a half of the series being on air, I think the viewing figures weren't what they hoped they would be and they started to offer me more and more money to go in. I wasn't having it but they just kept chucking money at me. I had no ambition to be in the jungle or go on reality TV but it got to the point where they were offering money I couldn't turn down.

It was a month's work maximum and I had a bit of an epiphany thinking about what my dad used to get paid and the days when I would help my mum out with her cleaning job. I can still recall my payslip at Woolies with £3.77 an hour on it. So I just couldn't, with a clear conscience, turn down the kind of money they were offering.

I could hear myself making all these excuses to the wider public about why I was doing it. I didn't want 'to go on a journey'. I'm not even bothered about being on TV, but it was a lot of money, so I went on.

It might sound a bit crazy to bring that back to normal life but every now and again you have to take on something that you don't want to do. You have to remind yourself you are supporting your family or earning some cash for something that really matters. There's no shame in taking work; life can be transactional and when you realise that, you can square a lot of conundrums away in your head.

Sometimes you get to a new job and for the first 20 minutes you're thinking, *I've got at least seven days of this. This is not happening, this is rubbish.* But you've still got to go through with it and perseverance is so important. You have to stick with things, you can't flounce out. *ALOTO* is the perfect example of that – I'm so grateful I stuck with it, despite the discomfort and awkwardness in the early days.

Woolworths was the same when I was a teenager. Getting out of bed, getting on my bike and cycling in when it was chucking it down? So many days I'd sooner have stayed in bed but I didn't and it's set me up for life.

I find it embarrassing now, some of the stuff that comes my way, where you think, *Wow, they're going to pay me that amount of money for this? I will do that, thank you very much.* It's a bit of everything – working-class values, looking after my family. It goes back to the trainers and the cars or measuring everything against what people got paid when I was younger. I remember hearing people talk about 'a salary' when I was young and I would hear the numbers being mentioned.

These days I can't turn opportunities down because I'm always measuring them against those early notions of money and value. Even when I give what I have earned away, I do it for that reason: I'd rather earn the money when it's on offer and find a good use for it. I know this life that I'm leading is not forever and I definitely don't want to work forever.

The strange thing about getting on in life is that my taste hasn't changed much. I don't want anything flashy, like clothes or watches. I really do have simple tastes and pleasures and I still can't believe the work I do can provide not just for me, but for my friends and family too.

Lockdown has created an industry for corporate Zoom events. I did a couple of them and really, all you're doing is sitting in your lounge answering questions and getting paid for it. I'm speaking to someone from a company, to all of the staff or whoever it is, and you just feel like at the end of it, you should offer them the money back because you can't believe there's a market for it. Though I have to say it actually works really well. I did one recently for Legal & General. It was so nice. Louis Theroux had done one, Olly Murs had been on singing and I bet they were pinching themselves as well. I hope they felt as good as I did. I was sat there, just having a lovely chat with the boss from his office. You completely forget there's an audience there and you're actually getting paid for it. The amazing thing is, they think they're getting a bargain because it's ever so slightly cheaper than what you'd do it for if you turned up in person. All of that said, I've not lost sight of what money is and what I used to earn and how I was brought up. If there's a market for it, then I can more than justify taking part.

It's very easy to get caught up in it all, where you get a bit pompous about jobs. When you talk about *Strictly* and reality TV, I don't think I'm above it. I might need them one day. If it all goes horribly wrong, then I might be doing the cha-cha-cha and why not? It's all a bit of a laugh.

I've had a good think about this and if I did *Strictly* (I'm NOT doing it), it would have to be with another bloke. It's got nothing to do with the so-called *Strictly* Curse, it would just be far more comfortable for me.

When they pick their partners, I find it the weirdest thing. But just imagine for a second, 'Here he is, former cricketer Freddie Flintoff. This year, you will be dancing with ... TREVOR!' I think I could handle that, no problem. I'd just wander over to Trev, have a handshake and off we go, let's get this thing going. Very business-like. Actually, let's go for Anton Du Beke and really break all the rules. I can just imagine it: 'Right, Anton, I'll lead you, son. Stick with me and keep up!' I reckon I could pick him up as well, no problem.

At least I'm safe for now from appearing on *Celebs Go Dating*, or a celebrity edition of *Naked Attraction*. There isn't enough money on earth to pay me for that curtain to be lifted and for the world to see my Hampton.

Top Gear

When Jeremy Clarkson left *Top Gear* in 2015, I told my agent that I would love to do that job. Thommo said that it was a good thing to aspire to but that it wasn't the right time, which was good advice. So I parked it and forgot about it. Then Matt LeBlanc was leaving in 2018 and there were going to be new presenters again. When Thommo told me in the corridor after filming *A League of Their Own* one night that I had a screen test, I got really competitive with it.

If there's something you really want in life, being passive is not the way to go. You have to find the competitive edge, develop an assertive attitude and be single-minded about getting it.

It was the first time in a long while I had really wanted a job. I told Thommo, 'If I don't get *Top Gear*, I'm close to knocking it all on the head and going back into cricket.' I did feel like I was at a crossroads.

I went to the screen test in Northampton at an RAF base and my first job was to do a test for a Dacia Duster, one of the cheapest new cars you can buy on the market. I'd seen all the stuff that they wanted me to say, but I made a decision that I was going to get this job by being myself or I would lose it that way. What I definitely won't do is tackle something in a style asked of me by somebody else, then feel bad about it. I'd never forgive myself if I had gone in and done it in a style I wasn't comfortable with, or in a way where I wasn't being authentic and lost it, so I told the team that I knew the script, I knew the car and I would do it as it came to me. I did exactly what I wanted to do and it went well.

When I got the job, it was a good feeling. Though I didn't enjoy doing the show that much to begin with because I had got so used to working with Jamie, Jack, Romesh and James on *ALOTO* and I was comfortable with them – they get me and they know me, they know my quirks and my social awkwardness. When I went into *Top Gear*, I was a bit scared to show that side of me, so I needed to put on a bit of bravado. We weren't who we really are to start with but now we're really comfortable with each other and we get on. It took some bedding in, some getting used to, but I'm enjoying it so much now – it's a dream gig.

When you retire from sport, it does feel like you're trying to recreate the dressing room wherever you go. We managed it on *ALOTO*, we're there now with *Top Gear*. Paddy gave me a bit of the dressing-room treatment recently – well, the closest you can get to one-upmanship possible in telly, similar to the way we would wind each other up in interviews when I was playing cricket. You would just leave a little remark in there that would be a subtle dig, but Paddy got me big time. I did a screen test, pilot and run-through for *Take Me Out* in Australia and in the early days of working with Paddy on *Top Gear*, I told him about it.

'You what? You did that?' he said.

Obviously in the UK, everyone knows Paddy as the host of *Take Me Out*, but I had to gently explain that no one knows who he is in Australia and I've done loads of work out there.

He was giving it the big one, saying he was going to do it but it clashed with something else. When I was doing the run-through, I found myself turning into Paddy McGuinness. I'd seen a fair bit of the show – it's a bit of a guilty pleasure of mine and my kids love it. I found myself mimicking him, saying stuff like, 'Let the barbie see the cue. Single man, reveal yourself.' I was even saying 'your' with his Bolton inflection, 'yoouur'. This was all before I knew I'd be working with Paddy and I wasn't sure I wanted the job anyway. When I found out I was going to be doing *Top Gear* with Pad, I took myself out the picture. So, I told him all about it and then in some promo he was doing, he embellished the story. He said, 'They wanted Fred for *Take Me Out Australia* but he was shit. They couldn't understand what he was saying, he was useless.'

Well played, Paddy. It's almost something I wish I had done myself, I had to doff my cap to him. Well played, sir. It made me laugh.

Not quite what I said, Paddy, but don't let that get in the way! He was rinsing me but it was funny and it definitely made me feel at home. We did the same to Chris Harris when we started a rumour he was joining *Strictly* and the whole thing grew arms and legs. Anyone who knows Chris will know how unrealistic that is.

I have to give them both a special mention here. Chris is such a brilliant lad as well. His knowledge and attention to detail on cars is on another level, his passion for the subject just oozes from him and I love working with him. With him and Paddy, I look forward to going to work and that has to be one of the things you can only dream of in your working life – they are great lads.

In July 2021, Paddy was announced as the new host of the BBC's *A Question of Sport* to replace Sue Barker, who had fronted the long-running quiz show for 24 years. I couldn't help but think, *how does he do it? Top Gear* was a surprise gig with our names on it, but *QoS*? Taking over from Sue and following in David Coleman's footsteps?

Paddy doing *QoS* is like me presenting *Newsnight* or standing in for Fiona Bruce on *Question Time*! The worst thing is, I bet Paddy will be good at it as well – and fair play to him. It's the reverse of the situation I get being a cricketer on an entertainment format, Paddy is an entertainer on a sport format. People get too precious about these things. Good luck to him. He'll have to put his tin hat on for a couple of weeks, but after that it'll all settle down.

Working with Your Heroes

Former Rangers star Ally McCoist is an incredible human being – he's a man who changes the temperature of every room he enters. I tell you what, I love that man. I remember when I first met him. To me, he was a massive personality – just charisma personified. When I was 20, I was a panellist on *A Question of Sport*. I was SO nervous, so I had a few drinks to settle my nerves, which didn't work – I just needed a wee. It was in the era of Ally and snooker's John Parrott as team captains and it was a prime time hit show.

Growing up, I watched *QoS* religiously, all the way back to when David Coleman was the host, with Bill Beaumont, Willie Carson and Emlyn Hughes as captains through to the Sue Barker era, and then suddenly I was a guest on the show. It's a bit embarrassing to admit, but despite all of those hours watching, I don't know anything about sport.

My mate, the cricketer, Gareth Davies wrote the questions on the show and he said, 'Don't worry, I've looked after you.' I didn't get one right! I was so nervous. There was a gag knocking about on the show where the captains would crowbar chocolate bars into the answers. So, John Parrott was giving it 'that's a small teaser, Sue' or s-Malteaser. Then Ally McCoist throws in, 'No need to Wispa, John.' I've got about ten of them in my head and I just didn't have the confidence to deliver. In my insecurity, I had just got a question wrong about Ian Botham and then I was asked Preston North End's nickname. Of course it's 'The Lilywhites', but I just froze. I wasn't even listening to the question properly because I was staring at Ally and John Parrott. I had no place getting into the showboating and humour, as much as the bullets were there ready to be fired. It was so frustrating. I was sat there with Ally, embarrassing myself.

I think one of the reasons I don't hit it off with many people is because I immediately think they don't like me. It's just the way I am, as Redknapp always reminds people. I'm sat there, thinking, *Ally doesn't like me because I can't get a question right. I'm not getting involved in the chocolate gags. He probably doesn't like cricket, he's Scottish. What am I doing here? I'm useless!* That was my inner monologue. And for most of my life that's been my thought process. But this is my life, my head, this is how it works.

I had always wanted to work with Ally again, so I was delighted when the chance came up to work on radio together. All the way through the first lockdown, I worked with him on talkSPORT – I admit I was a bit nervous because I was starstruck again.

The morning slot on radio is punishing. I assumed it

would be great to have the whole day to yourself after you've finished, but you're constantly tired, it's like having jet lag. You promise yourself you'll get to bed early and even when you do, you can't sleep because you're thinking about how early you have to be up the next day.

I used to get up in the morning so angry because I hadn't been able to sleep from worrying about the show. Then I'd get my laptop fired up and Ally McCoist would be on my screen and he's got his phone up showing me his garden because there was a deer in it that morning. He's got the views, the snow. Ally's one of the most enthusiastic human beings on planet Earth. I'm openly jealous of him, his sunny disposition and his zest for life. It's infectious. He's brilliant.

Sometimes I feel like I'm stuck when I was Andrew Flintoff, aged 20. I still like Nike Air Jordan trainers, because they were so good when I was that age. I like Ferrari 355s because that was the best car when I was going into my third decade. And Ally McCoist – he was such a big personality back then, I still place him on a pedestal. Ally was the first proper entertainment broadcaster I was aware of who had crossed over from sport, where he was universally loved. Although he was in a movie with Robert Duvall (*A Shot at Glory*, 2000), now that was dodgy – it wasn't all perfect!

Pundits

I got quite a bit of stick when I was hosting talkSPORT Breakfast with Ally and Laura Woods during the pandemic. The strange thing about working in sport as a broadcaster is that the criticism does get to me.

By contrast, with *Top Gear*, 5 million people will watch and you see all the comments on Twitter, most of them about how we aren't as good as Jeremy Clarkson, Richard Hammond and James May and I can just dust over it, I'm not even bothered. I don't even care, I find it amusing. I'm even thinking about retweeting some of it. There's a brilliant meme knocking about of Clarkson, where he's shouting 'Rubbish!', which gets reeled out so many times. It's a clip of him, disgusted about something, and people reply to our content or our remarks online with that meme every single time. I don't even know Jeremy, though I'd like to meet him. It's all just a bit of fun, but that trick on social media has run out of steam now – the trolls need a new one.

When it comes to my TV work for cricket, where I think I've achieved a lot in the game, I get a bit of abuse. It's a completely different experience on radio.

On talkSPORT I got shit for being a cricketer discussing football. Then I got shit for talking about cricket, so you can't win with a certain audience. It's ruthless. I'm glad social media wasn't around when I was playing – I would have been fined every week for reacting to trolls, I just wouldn't have been able to bite my tongue at that stage of my life.

I don't care who you are or how resilient you are, it still needles you. I didn't read the press when I was playing, but somehow you still see what is being said about you. It would get through to you and that still hurts.

Trolling is something that we really need to address in society, even on the milder side of it when people feel comfortable re-tweeting cruel thoughts and views. A lot of it just isn't funny and it should be called out properly in the time we're living in.

I've had to take it on the chin since I was a teenager, so I've been conditioned to criticism all my life, but if you are thrust into fame, it's a heavy thing to deal with. The worst thing is you reach a point of acceptance, which simply shouldn't be the case. I'm talking about schoolkids being bullied online, or all the abuse you saw after England missed some penalties in the Euros. Something has to be done about it.

As much as you hear me say I'm relaxed about things, I do work at improving as a presenter and I work hard. Often, I still don't completely understand when I get a job why I've landed it. I've seen clips of myself hosting things and I can barely bring myself to watch it back.

Every year, I see pro sportsmen and women becoming

pundits and presenters and you can't help but draw a comparison with your own experience. I adopt a sporting mentality: I watch and listen to see who is doing the same stuff as me. They say you should never compare yourself to others, it only ever leads to unhappiness, which is all very well in theory, but looking at the people you admire, respect or hold in high esteem and seeing what you can do to emulate or improve on that benchmark can be useful. Just try not to compare yourself with others on social media!

England's second-highest wicket-taker Darren Gough is on talkSPORT in the afternoons and I can tell he is well researched – that's where punditry has changed in recent history. He loves it, he's really engaging on air. I love Goughie. Talk about someone who could have had an amazing career but never had their best years because of injuries. If it wasn't for that, he might have done the same as Jimmy Anderson. That good without having his best years, it's bonkers!

I look at *Match of the Day* as a masterclass of broadcasting. Gary Lineker is a brilliant presenter and the rapport he has with Alan Shearer and Ian Wright is outstanding. I watched *MOTD* recently when they were covering the FA Cup and I had to tweet about it afterwards because it was so good. There was no ego, just three blokes having a laugh while breaking the game down. I was learning from them, I felt like they were educating me at the same time as entertaining me, which was one of the founding principles of the BBC when it started. It was a different class. With some pundits, they'll just describe a good pass or a good goal. I want to know why it happened. I want an explanation of how someone created that space or moved players around the pitch with certain passes to unlock a chance.

As a kid, I was never really into football but I absolutely love it now. I've really got into it through my sons and we love watching it together. I particularly love the derbies – Rangers v Celtic, Hibs v Hearts (I'm 20 per cent Scottish after all!), Preston v Blackpool, a couple of them Scandinavian teams (because I'm a Viking), anyone!

When I was younger, I played a couple of games for Preston North End Boys Club and I was scouted by Blackburn. The manager told me a scout had been and asked for my name, and I just replied 'Why?'. I was under no illusions I was any good. Just a big lad at the back – they probably based the decision on my physical presence. I knew what they were after! Football never clicked in my head the same way cricket did. I'd look at a game and I really didn't know what I was doing. With cricket, from a really young age, I could see it all unfold and read the game.

I like listening to Jamie on Sky Sports and I've become a big admirer of Alex Scott. I think she's a great pundit and a class act as well – especially in the face of the criticism and abuse she gets online. She's played at the top level in football for a good amount of time and she's clearly diligent with her research and preparation.

I watched her present *The One Show* the other week and the biggest compliment I could give her is that I didn't see an ex-footballer, I just saw a presenter of *The One Show*.

I was doing an interview – and this sounds really wanky, I know – for BAFTA and we got on to the subject of former sportsmen and women working as broadcasters. I will always stand up for ex-sportsmen because as a sportsperson, you've come into entertainment and everyone jumps on you. There are a lot of voices asking why you have the job: is it just because he played sport? I understand turning the television on and seeing me can be hard for them, but that's fine because at some point my face won't fit and someone else will step in.

I see former England striker Peter Crouch doing *Save Our Summer* – which was a bit ambitious for a title in the midst of the pandemic – and people were hammering him. I thought he was brilliant. He was Peter Crouch, completely genuine and true to himself. The uncomfortable bits when he was doing his link to camera, he's in it with you. You know it's uncomfortable and he's telling you he's laughing with you as he trips up here and there.

People like me and Crouchie, we know there are better presenters out there than us but that's their main profession and always has been. I would sooner watch Crouchie being Crouchie than him attempting to be a slick host. I'm not going to be slick like Dermot O'Leary at the BAFTAs or David Jones on Sky Sports when he's presenting *Super Sunday* or *Monday Night Football*. They are both brilliant presenters, but I never want to compete with them. I don't consider myself to be a presenter, I turn up and do my thing, but I don't think of myself in the same bracket.

I think that's something that extends to every walk of life: you have to be true to yourself. The idea that you suddenly have to behave in a certain way because of perceived pressure or what you assume is required of you isn't helpful – that diminishes what got you there in the first place.

Tracksuits and Trainers

My mum always said to me, 'Under my roof, three things you're not having; an earring, a tattoo and a motorbike.' Sorry, Mum. I ended up getting all three though I've lost my bottle on motorbikes.

Nothing said showbiz like that diamond earring! I put one on the other week for *Top Gear* when we did a thing about midlife crises and I felt like a tit. I had it in my ear and I could just feel it all the time, making me so self-conscious everywhere I went. I found myself explaining it to everyone – 'Oh, for filming this. *Filming.*'

I remember getting it done in Nottingham. It was during a Test match week and Rob Key had one so I decided I'd have it, too. I was stood in the queue at Claire's Accessories in Nottingham with Rob, Steve Harmison and about ten 13-year-old girls.

Most shows I work on have a clothing budget. As the jobs have improved, so have the clothes – at least the jewellery has calmed down a bit. The more I've worked and knocked around with Jamie Redknapp, the more I've thought about what I wear. We get given a certain amount of money to spend on outfits for the show. If you go into Jamie's room, he's got a rail and it'll have four tops to choose from for the budget. If you go to mine, I've got my clothes for the year!

Top Gear also provide us with our wardrobe, but I don't feel quite as much pressure stood next to Chris Harris. And definitely not next to Paddy! With the game shows on top, I'm getting three or four wardrobes a year, which is brilliant. I take it all home and my cupboards are bursting at the seams. I find it really hard to get rid of anything. It's stuff I couldn't afford when I was younger and I appreciate the value in it, and I know what it costs. For that reason, I struggle to give it away, especially because not many people are my size. My dad will have some of it, though my brother lives abroad, so he misses out. I took 15 bags to the charity shop the other day because they could sell it and make some good money.

WORK

At the same time though, in terms of fashion, if left to my own devices, I've got about as much range as Steve Irwin, the late Crocodile Hunter guy. I've got five identical tracksuits and the best I can do for flair is my Imelda Marcos-esqe collection of shoes – well, trainers to be precise. If you're too young to know who she is, I'm sure she'll be the first name to pop up if you Google 'extravagant shoe collections'.

When I see Harry Styles being bold enough to embrace really mad outfits, I know the 20-year-old me would be hammering him for it. If I'd had Twitter, I would have been digging him out. And here's the thing, and it seems to surprise a lot of people, but this 43-year-old thinks, *That really suits you, son. Why not?* I would have been far too fearful of the negative comments to be as bold as Harry at his age, regardless of how much money there is in his bank account. In fact, I'm a bit envious of that freedom of expression and how I'm only getting to a position of comfort with it now.

I always find myself thinking about being on my way to that point where you truly are your real self. You have found the confidence to wear stuff like Harry without fear of criticism or ridicule.

On the last series of *Top Gear*, I started wearing tinted glasses around the studio and on camera. I knew it would cause a stir and they would try to discourage me from wearing them because as soon as you put on a pair of glasses with a tint they go into meltdown. What they didn't realise was that I had three different tints, all lined up in anticipation of my next move.

I played them like a fiddle when they said they liked my glasses but the dark tint was too dark to go on film. That was fine because I had the same frames in a really light tint. Clyde Holcroft, one of our writers, asked, 'Are you going to watch the first episode of this series when it goes on?'

I said, 'No. But I am going to watch Twitter for the glasses' comments!'

Oh, I wasn't let down, was I heck!

Back to Cricket?

When people have had enough of what I do, I'll give it up and move on. I'm always toying with the idea of returning to cricket in some capacity, so I never have the same fear of failure on telly, which is a privilege I'm grateful for. It's a huge pressure removed, knowing I have a Plan B. I know I'm in a luxurious position career wise, but it's worth considering change if you're not happy and you can see another option to make life better. If you can't, spending time exploring the route out of a career cul-de-sac is time well spent.

Eventually, I think I would like to work in cricket again in some capacity. I've signed up to present the new format for Sky, The Hundred. For me, it's a way of dipping my toe in the water again with a fresh new competition. Rob Key is probably my biggest pull because he's doing every game with me. I'll get to spend time with one of my closest mates and I know we will love it. The best thing will be taking my kids – they will love it. Having them around is something I'm really looking forward to.

The other reason I'm determined to make a success of it is because this competition is going to cost the game so much money, it has to work. And if me being there helps, then why not? If it attracts new fans or encourages some of the fans the sport has lost to come back, then game on!

Coming Out of Retirement . . . Briefly

I played cricket in April 2021 with my son Corey. He's 15 now. He got picked for St Annes first team.

I was at practice on the Thursday before a game and they were struggling for numbers a bit. I told them I would put my kit in the car in case they just wanted someone to field so they took that as coming out of retirement to play in the first team! It's not a brilliant side but it's not bad; each side has a professional they pay.

It was Corey's debut for the first team so he was a bit nervous. We were thinking he would bat number six and I was thinking I'd be ten to make up the numbers. But next thing, they asked if I'll bat at six. They were playing against Morecambe and I've not played at that ground since I was 17. Almost 25 years later and there are still a few of the same faces knocking about.

Luckily, they were so nice. I went in after Corey and I was pissed off, not with him, but because I wanted to bat with him. Instead, I was going out to bat crossing him.

I was upset he was out because he was off the pitch, which wasn't the plan. I'm trying my nuts off, but I just couldn't do it and managed three runs. I'm chatting to the opposition, they were sound. I had no right to score any runs because I've not picked a bat up for four years and I don't practise, I don't play at all. But I just can't handle not being able to do something. So I came off and I pretended I wasn't bothered. But I was absolutely seething. Fucking seething! I sat down and I laughed it off and we got beaten, but it was a nice day.

It was 50 overs a side so I was fielding for four hours. Just stood there. The next day, I was completely cream crackered. It was a reminder that as much as I love the notion of still playing, my body just isn't up to it.

CHAPTER FOUR

FRIENDSHIP

'They had straws in the top and were cracking into it like it was Vimto.'

How to Tell Who Your Proper Mates Are

I can tell you a story about true friendship. An incident that proves who you really care about because a more passing acquaintance or relationship would definitely end as a result of what I'm about to tell you.

The carnage that followed The Ashes win in 2005 has been written about so extensively you'd think there would be nothing left to chew over, especially when it comes to the boozing involved. So much was written about that session, the whole thing grew arms and legs.

After the game, I stayed in the hotel with a few mates for a while to celebrate with familiar faces. Oddly, there was one person involved who we didn't know too well, the son of someone I had met through cricket. This guy's dad is incredibly wealthy – off-the-scale rich. Looking back, I don't actually know how he ended up with us because he was more a friend of a friend. Fair play to him for getting involved in the celebrations, you can only admire that behaviour – it was a momentous occasion.

As a thank you for taking him under our wing, his dad sent me an incredible case of red wine: Penfolds Grange, 1981. The date was significant because it was the last time England won The Ashes. There were six bottles in the case and a conservative estimate would put the price at around a few hundred quid per bottle. As you can imagine, I tucked it away for a really special occasion but I made sure it was kept at the perfect temperature ready for when the time was right.

I came back from a tour of India on Christmas Eve that year and Rachael had organised a surprise party. If the truth be told, I was a bit pissed when I got off the plane and was looking forward to getting back so I could get my head down. I got back and everyone was at my house already getting into a big sesh. All my mates were there and it was actually a really touching moment. Everyone was well-oiled, all the drink was put on for them. I had some wine coolers in the garage and I said, in my half-cut wisdom to one of the lads, 'Go and get whatever you want.'

The next thing, I looked round and four of my best mates had a bottle of the Penfolds Grange each. Not only that, they had straws in the top and were cracking into it like it was Vimto. Four Preston lads, nodding to me, going, 'Hey, it's all right, this gear, y'know!'

Fucking right it was! I never even told them – it was too late anyway and that's what happens when you invite Preston lads round for a drink. They will drink whatever they get their hands on and ask questions later. I didn't want them feeling bad either and, actually, it was the perfect way for the wine to be drunk. Those lads were loving it so fair play to them. I got the last two bottles and tucked in with them – I didn't use a straw, mind you, that would be taking the piss.

It's something I've learned over the years: you can't get uptight about stuff like that. If anything, there's something amazing about enjoying the spoils of your trade with real pals. It's not quite the same on your own, it's better to share a lot of that stuff. Within reason, right enough: it has to be with proper mates.

Work Mates

ALOTO's Romesh Ranganathan and Tom Davis have become proper friends. I think our common ground is that we all had a life before we found fame, or notoriety, or whatever you want to call it. Tom was a doorman, a scaffolder, a drag queen and sold T-shirts with insulting logos at Glastonbury before he made it on telly. Romesh sold sunglasses at Gatwick Airport. He was a teacher, too.

I think when people meet Tom, like they do with me sometimes, they expect a big hooligan. But he's so far the opposite: he's gentle, he's kind, he's just a lovely man. I remember I was sat in the writing room and we were talking about people to come on the show and Fraser Steele, one of the writers, knew Tom. He mentioned Tom and said we'd all get on really well. Tom is just a nice bloke, he's someone's company I feel comfortable in. I trust him implicitly.

Big Tom is the same off-air as he is on it. He puts his arm around me and he's one of the few people on the planet big enough for me to just nuzzle under his wing. For the size of him and the look of him, he's got his insecurities as well, which he's open about and I admire him for that, too.

The fact I can be quite quiet annoys some people. If I've got nothing to say, I'm not going to say anything and I don't enter conversations I don't know anything about. For me, that's a measure of my comfort with people, when I'm sat there in someone's company not feeling I need to speak or do anything. I always have that with Rom – I just enjoy his company, it's just so easy. He also happens to be an incredibly funny man.

When Romesh first came on *A League of Their Own* in 2015, I got him on. And that was only because my brother-in-law worked with him in Sunglass Hut at Gatwick Airport. He was saying to me, 'Have you seen this Romesh Ranganathan lad knocking about on the telly? He's a brilliant lad. I used to work with him at the airport and he's a funny man.' After that, I asked the producers to get him on and he was everything I was hoping he would be. He was so good. We're on WhatsApp to each other a few days every week. Even though we don't talk in person so much, we are still really close friends.

Then there's the crocked former footballer and former face of Thomas Cook holidays, Jamie Redknapp. Give him his due, he was a really good footballer, but he has had to find a second career as a broadcaster, like I have.

I think back to the early days of *A League of Their Own* when I was still well and truly into my drinking. I was sat there, all 19 stone of me, and you've got that Adonis of a man sitting across from you? Imagine. It would wobble even the most confident bloke. And I wobbled a lot back then, in every sense.

We spend a lot of time together and he's forever throwing me under the bus with people for a laugh. He does it every time. He'll introduce me to them and say, 'This is Fred. It took him eight years to return my phone calls, so don't be offended if he fucks you off. He's like that, don't be put off.'

It's true that it's only in the past few years we have become really good mates. I was in awe of Jamie a little bit. He's so good-looking, you can't help but feel inferior. It was a tough friendship to start with. I would wonder if he was my mate, did he like me? But in recent years, and I don't know if it's because I started combing my hair, he's become a proper mate. Jamie is brilliant, he's one of my closest mates now and you can't help but respect how talented he was as a footballer, which is often forgotten when we are mucking about on the show. He was top, top class.

I'm not going to lie, I have started trying a bit harder with the way I look, especially when I'm in his company. I put a bit of 'smelly' on and then I look at the clothes I've worn afterwards, thinking, *I've pushed the boat out.* The truth is, I haven't compared to him. It comes so naturally to him, white suits at Wembley aside.

The Road Trip with *ALOTO* changed the game for us. Spending so much time together away from home for three weeks really helped our relationships develop, we got to know each other so well.

We really didn't know what to expect on the trip. The premise was James Corden taking us to America, where he had landed the gig hosting *The Late Late Show* for CBS. Me, Jack Whitehall and Jamie flew out and James set us a series of tasks, which got more adventurous and bigger in scale in each episode. Massively jet lagged, we started off with a tenpin bowling challenge, which was a walk in the park for me. But then the true scale of it hit me when we found ourselves attempting 'field goal kicking' at an Oakland Raiders game in front of a huge crowd. We were all used to playing in front of big crowds but that was something else. By the end of the first episode we were swimming from Alcatraz back to San

Francisco – the water genuinely has sharks in it and it's not an easy swim in choppy waters.

I've seen it on Discovery – there are species of shark you haven't even heard of kicking about that stretch of water AND Great Whites. As we were going in, they told us it wasn't true. Once we were in the water we could see some splashing in the distance and thank God it was only a seal – but that's not what your head tells you when you're in there. So we got through it and two weeks after we got home, it was all over the press that there was a Great White shark attack at Alcatraz. They even had CCTV of this beast taking a seal – I watched it! And here's the thing: if a Great White was knocking about that day, who's he going to take? Jamie's old, leathery and tough, and as for Jack, there's not a meal in him – I'd be done for!

The experiences were mind-blowing. We drove in actual NASCAR vehicles and then, a few days later, we were onstage in Vegas as extras in Cirque du Soleil's show *Zarkana*. Jamie played an apple seller in *Aladdin* on Broadway, putting in a proper performance. It's madness – Jamie Redknapp on Broadway? I'm laughing right now.

Whoever lost the challenges was at risk of appearing on stage in Vegas with The Chippendales and the thought of it was terrifying. We're all game for a laugh but Jamie was definitely the most nervous about it – you could tell because he wanted to win the challenges.

When I lost, I had to take to the stage with The Chippendales so I just completely went for it! All out, no shame, writhing around on the stage doing The Worm, pumping my hips. I actually think I got away with it – I reckon if it all goes tits up, there's another life for me in Vegas with the lads.

During that trip a real bond developed between us. We went for dinner, me Jamie, Jack and James. Afterwards, we went to see Seinfeld live and somehow after that ended up in Calvin Harris' DJ booth at Hakkasan on the strip in Vegas. EDM is not my cup of tea, but that night, I was loving it. I was standing with Jack and Jamie. James is dancing about, which he always does, and then Calvin swans in, says hello and shakes our hands, but then he's straight into his job. He doesn't make any eye contact with anyone, just looks at his decks, the audience, finishes his gig, then goes off. He was with Taylor Swift at the time and the spotlight was really on him. After that, we watched Jamie lose a bit of money on the tables at the casino. He told us he'd been there before, so we watched him stick a lump on red – and lose! I think I got to bed about 6am, I was genuinely shattered. We were filming scenes the next day in dark glasses. I had stopped drinking by that point in my life but the rest of the lads were getting wired in properly.

It's no coincidence that *A League of Their Own* started to fly once we'd been on that first trip away together and that was down to understanding more about each other – knowing when we could push each other's buttons and when to step back. Perhaps that's something we could all learn from? In team sport, in business, some time away from where the actual work happens can really help develop bonds. I know most folk go on an away day but I think a week would really sort things out. Take everyone to Vegas and see what happens! Well, maybe not the best idea right now, it being currently on the amber list, but you get my point. Get off to Camber Sands or Skeggy instead!

When I first met Jack Whitehall on the show in 2010, I was sceptical about this spotty 20-year-old posh lad, though he made us all laugh. It was amazing how quickly he won us all over. He knew James really well and I think that's how he got involved. I got on really well with him, so we got him back on for two episodes in that run of *ALOTO* and the rest is history. He made that role on the show his and he was such a big part of taking the series forwards.

He got a bit upset when we were in the car on the Road Trip. Jamie kept bringing his book everywhere to get it plugged during the show so I got one of mine sent, not for the show, just to have a chat about and to show them.

Jack took it and he was reading a passage from it, then he goes to the index at the back to find his name. I don't think he had a lot of numbers after his name and his bottom lip popped out in a huff. Then he looks for Romesh and Jamie and they had loads of mentions. I actually felt really bad because it was completely unintentional. So, Jack, now you're ignoring the rest of the book and looking up your mention, hello!

Jack made a series a couple of years back for BBC1, *Jack Whitehall's Sporting Nation*. It was presented as a monologue, with him waxing lyrical about some household names. He filmed bits about Seb Coe, Steve Ovett, Dame Kelly Holmes, Sir Steve Redgrave and a few others. In the trailer, he made some flippant remark, teasing an upcoming show with the line, 'The show features our greatest sporting heroes: *Sir* Andy Murray, *Dame* Kelly Holmes, *Top Gear*'s Freddie Flintoff, apparently he played cricket . . .' He just mugged me off so I didn't watch it because I thought it was going to be a massive piss-take. Then we had a bit of chat on WhatsApp, where he was asking me if I'd watched it and I eventually gave in.

I watched it with my family. It was something like a ten-minute montage, quite heartfelt, from Jack about my career. I didn't expect it and was sat there with the kids and it was the weirdest thing because I've never looked back on my playing days with them. They were all so impressed by it and I got a bit of a lump in my throat. I texted Jack to tell him I didn't expect it and to say a heartfelt thanks, and to our other mate, Clyde Holcroft, who wrote the show with Jack. It was really touching and I hadn't thought Jack

FRIENDSHIP

would do something so poignant, considering we spend most of the time winding each other up. He replied and said, 'To be honest with you, I was a kid when you were doing all that. It was such a special time in my life.' I just don't see myself as anything like that and though I sat next to him on the show all those times, it had never occurred to me he would be a fan of me as a player. I love Jack, he's brilliant, but I didn't think he was that bothered.

When we were doing the most recent Road Trip, up in Scotland in 2020, I had a moment when we were trudging through the hills having a laugh and I realised how much I enjoyed being around Jack, Jamie and Romesh. They've become proper mates and Jack just brings something special to the show, but more importantly, he's brilliant to be around.

James Corden is doing so well for himself, it's unreal. The stratospheric rise of his career has been something to behold and he's a really hard-working lad, though it's often easy to forget that he's a brilliant actor first of all. When he starred in *One Man Two Guv'nors* in 2011 at the Festival Theatre in London, he won every award going, including Tonys when they took it to Broadway. But, in the interests of balance, *Cats* didn't do so well in the cinema! These days I don't see him so much because he lives in LA, but I'm looking forward to spending time with him again because the moments when we are together are special – he's a really good lad, James.

We all went to his wedding in September 2012. The number of famous faces who showed up was incredible, it seemed like everyone who was anyone was there. We were only invited as evening guests but it was no wonder when you saw how many people James had befriended! Tom Daley the diver was there, having a vol-au-vent with Kylie Minogue.

It was bonkers.

The thing with James I have to give him credit for is how he never loses touch with us all. I messaged him about doing a video to help the Manchester Children's Hospital with their fundraising and he got back to me in two minutes. It's amazing to see how far he has gone, and Jack is the same.

I was so pleased when Jack came back for the Road Trip in Scotland, so he could spend time with us. He had just done a movie (*Jungle Cruise*) with Dwayne 'The Rock' Johnson! One thing about both of them is they are completely fearless. You usually associate that attribute with rugby players, boxers or even footballers entering a hostile stadium.

In TV, James and Jack have this incredible bottle to walk out in front of thousands of people and be completely at ease. I'd be lying if I said I've not learned from them during those experiences. It's about putting yourself in terrifying situations and surviving. I've learned from them how to handle that. That, and their insane work ethic – real grafters, they've earned every bit of success that has come their way.

Losing Friends

When I retired and we moved to Dubai in 2009 I naturally lost contact with quite a lot of people. We just nipped off with no fanfare to start again – we didn't even have somewhere to live arranged, we just took off.

I took a lot of criticism when we were beaten 5–0 in The Ashes in 2007. It felt like I was being obliterated by everyone around that time, it was grim. I think partly it was because we had set high expectations following 2005 but it still felt like the punishment dished out was incredibly severe for under-performing in Australia.

Worst of all, people I thought would reach out when I hit a career low never got in contact. That was a significant moment in my life and since then, my circle of friends has become so much smaller, which I actually really like. It's a good barometer of your proper friendships, to see who gets in touch when your circumstances change dramatically.

I've made plenty of mistakes when it comes to friendships, too. One of my best pals growing up was a lad called Tajinder. He should have been at my wedding in London but my head was in the wrong place to remember how important he had been to me when I was a kid.

The day before the wedding, I had treated some of the lads to a day out. We went for dinner at Asia de Cuba at St Martin's

Lane Hotel and then on to the Light Bar for drinks afterwards in the hotel upstairs.

When I was outside at one point, I bumped into Tajinder. I remember this happiness when I saw him and giving him a big hug. We were having a chat and it reminded me he was such a lovely lad. He'd gone completely bald and I was winding him up about it.

He introduced me to his girlfriend and I remember thinking I should invite them to the wedding on the spot. For some reason, I didn't. We were really tight on numbers but that's just an excuse. The other was, I was on the verge of being a bit pissed. I was standing, swaying about, so I wasn't in the frame of mind to make a decision like that without Rachael being involved.

I just don't know why I didn't do it. It's probably down to my social awkwardness again. I'm going to look him up soon because I really want to catch up with him properly. I'm still cross with myself because I told myself we were tight on numbers but he's too important to me to have left out and I need to fix that.

Mates as You Get Older

As I've said, I've found that as I've got older, I don't have as many friends as I used to. The ones I do have around me now will be with me for the rest of my days though.

My best mate in the world is Paddy McKeown. We joined

FRIENDSHIP

Lancashire at the same time and we speak or text every day. Regardless of what happens to me, I know Paddy will always be there for me. It would have to be something seriously outrageous for us to fall out. That's a life lesson in friendship – you know the ones that will survive.

Me and Paddy were joined together at the hip when we were at Lancashire, but looking back, I've not always been the best of friends to him. For a while I was too wrapped up in my own thing and also too proud to go to him with my problems, which I regret.

I trust him implicitly. I know exactly how he feels towards me and it's reciprocated. I can be myself around him – he knows me as me and not this telly person. He takes me for who I really am, with all my faults and everything, as I do with him. It's amazing, really.

There are so many unspoken things men don't do, especially when it comes to our emotions and being too proud to open up a bit. There are people who could have helped me at my lowest ebb and he's one of them, but we couldn't be in a better place right now.

In some ways, I'm a closed shop and I didn't realise how much some people actually like me and the result of that is often reflected in my behaviour towards them. But I laugh now as I can find the humour in it because I seem to be in awkward scrapes all the time.

If you see me on *A League of Their Own*, I think I come across as an extrovert. The truth is, I'm really introverted. As a result of that, I'll often say stupid things when I first meet people, which can sound quite rude. Because I'm aware of it, I just shut up and keep quiet. It's not quite Tourette's but I'll often say the first thing that comes into my head. I've heard it can often happen to taller people – I notice Crouchy (Peter Crouch) does it. And he'll stoop down a bit so he doesn't appear so conspicuous. I do the same because I'm quite big and can be loud – I have to check myself so it doesn't sound like a giant shouting at people.

If you only meet me once, there's a chance you'll file the experience under unusual and awkward, so that's probably why it has affected my ability to develop more friendships over the years. Those who have persevered, through choice or a contractual obligation, they are the ones that have survived.

It's funny how you look at people differently with age and hindsight and a bit more wisdom. When I was younger, playing professional sport, I thought everyone should think like me. I thought everyone outside of sport was a bit weird. I just couldn't fathom why other people didn't want to do what I was doing. But I look at my mates now who I muck about with and I just like having people there who I can look to and they know me not for the person who's on the

FRIENDSHIP

telly or presenting, just the awkward bag of bones and skin from Preston.

Donald McInnes, who works as a make-up artist on the shows I do, has been there with me since day one in TV. He's the best in the business when it comes to make-up and hair. He does make-up and sorts my hair, but just having him around means so much more. He's become a really close mate. If you said to either of us at school that we would eventually become really close friends, we would have laughed. But that's another beautiful aspect of maturity and experience – the people who become such a big part of life are often the most unlikely. Those surprises make life so interesting and I've taken real pleasure from those blossoming friendships.

Clyde Holcroft, who I've worked with for years, has also become a really good mate. I just love having him there – and not just because he's an absolutely brilliant writer but our friendship gives me the confidence to do my job. He's always been there for me.

In 2017, I did a show for ITV called *All Star Musicals* with West End legend Michael Crawford, the actor Tony Robinson and former Olympian Denise Lewis, amongst others. I hosted the show from the London Palladium and it was completely ridiculous as you would expect, with over-the-top musical theatre. At one point, I was stood at the top of some stairs on the stage with a curtain draped across me, dressed in the full *Phantom of the Opera* gear, mask and all. I even had the bloody cloak on. The next moment, I heard the announcer say, 'Host of the show, Freddie Flintoff!' followed by the music and then the curtains drawing back . . . I came down the stairs, whipped the mask off and I started the opening bars of one of the most famous musicals on the planet. Who did I think I was? I'm sure the audience wanted someone like Fred Astaire not Fred Flintoff.

Before we went on, I shared a knowing glance with Clyde. We didn't need to say anything, we were both laughing in the knowledge we had the same question on the tips of our tongues – 'What the actual fuck is going on?' Everyone was treating it so seriously, so having Clyde there to laugh along with me at the ridiculousness of the situation was massive.

There I am, trying to sing and dance like Gene Kelly. Jazz hands and moving a cane around like I knew what I was doing, but I was dying inside. I remember the relief afterwards – I'd done it in front of a full Palladium, a venue that I knew from the telly as a kid.

Just as my nerves had settled down and having killed some of the finest songs in musical history, unfortunately they asked me to do it again. They wanted some more camera angles, but in my head that was a call for 'that was shit'.

The second time I finished, I walked to Clyde who was standing at the side of the stage. He tried to offer me words

FRIENDSHIP

of comfort by saying well done. I saw straight through it, and my natural reaction to Clyde, as much as I love him, was to say 'fuck off'.

To make matters even worse, Michael Crawford was actually there, the original Phantom! I knew him and loved him as the accident-prone Frank Spencer in the BBC's classic comedy *Some Mothers Do 'Ave 'Em* and he was so lovely to me, he was everything I wanted him to be. We did a run-through and he had a big part in the show.

When he came out on stage, he got a standing ovation and you could see the tears in his eyes, which was lovely. It was a really nice moment, which more than made up for my terrible attempt at singing.

When the show went out on Christmas Eve, it was well received and was commissioned as a series. At that point though, they got John Barrowman in! I was pied off completely, but I think it was probably for the best.

I've become really good friends with a lad called Stan, who is now a fitness instructor and I train with him. He gets on really well with my kids and it's no wonder because he's closer to them in age than he is to me – he's only 24 and I'm 43. Even though I was a professional cricketer for all those years, I feel like he is educating me all the time. Maybe it's because he's old before his time and miserable like me, but he's such a good kid.

It's one of the loudest things I can shout from this book, to be open to other people and what they stand for and believe in. You don't have to agree on everything – the dynamics of disagreeing play such a big part in a healthy relationship. It's why I can't get my head around cancel culture – or immediately striking people out of your existence because they feel differently about politics or the latest story in the news. That just doesn't compute in my head. If you only surround yourself with people who have exactly the same views, surely that's odd? It would be pretty boring if you agreed on everything all the time, too. What a dull existence that would be.

The importance of the support from people I know and trust is something that took me a long time to appreciate properly. It's one thing that helps me thrive and it's why I sometimes struggled with making a debut or moving to a new team.

When I was playing cricket, I learned that I needed a few people I'm really close to because that gives me a more valuable reason for doing something. I had to share those massive experiences with people close to me to fully enjoy it. With hindsight, I needed those people in defeat as much as victory. It's in the dark times when you really find out who your friends are. If I felt like we were just men paid to turn up to play, that wasn't enough to drive a big performance. It had to mean more than that. Blood and thunder, real toil and emotion – it was all required to stir up the passion in me to succeed.

FRIENDSHIP

Playing for England and what that meant was so important to me, I've still got the tattoos to prove it. Also, playing for Lancashire and having that commitment to the club where I drive up to the ground and they still have my pictures up – that means everything to me. I feel like I belong there. I was always proud to play for Lancashire and England, I was never bored.

I also need people I am close to or I trust. Having Harmy there for most of my career, or Rob Key, that just made it even more special, having that shared experience. I enjoy their success just as much as mine. It was so good when it was the three of us.

I remember with Goughie and Mark Butcher having that feeling, too. People I trusted and knew I could share it all with. You are thrown together because of cricket, not because you are friends. I had really close mates, team-mates I got on well with but didn't see out of the game. And I had people I didn't like, which was inevitable.

When I was bowling or batting, playing well, I wasn't doing it for me, I was doing it for Harmy, the lads and the fans who had paid to follow us around the world. When he got 7 for 13 in the West Indies and bowled them out, I felt like I did it too. And when Keysey got 231 at Lord's, I got more excited than when I did something special.

When it gets to the dark times, in real life, sport or TV, you really find out who matters. When everything is going well, everyone wants to be your mate, but that's not when you really need people. It's when you're struggling or not doing so well that you need a good group of people to help.

When the music stops, everyone goes home. Footballers suffer more than anyone. Everyone wants your money when you're at the top, everyone wants to earn off you. I was ripped off by people I thought were friends and I will never make that mistake again – I'm more of a closed shop now.

I'm not a great talker, I'm not good at small talk or having really big opinions on stuff I don't know enough about, but I do like to listen to people and learn. To find my feet, I need to be surrounded by the right personalities. It's stating the obvious, but it extends to every walk of life – you need to identify collaborative, helpful people as quickly as possible when you enter a new environment. Ask yourself who will have your back, go out of their way to support you and is that someone you would reciprocate the favour for?

So, who are the people in *your* life that you wouldn't mind drinking the best booze in your house through a straw?

CHAPTER FIVE

FAILURE AND SUCCESS

'Michael Jordan wouldn't have been the sporting icon he is, if he had been a people pleaser.'

Hard Graft

Failing was such a strong, horrible emotion when I played cricket because winning meant everything to me. I've not experienced the same gut-wrenching, obsessive fury in any other walk of life than I did when I lost a game of cricket. I can be on telly, say the wrong thing or muck up a link and that's nowhere near as severe an emotion as the one I felt in failure on the field.

I can accept failure up until a point, but I can't accept not trying. All the times I did badly or we lost, I knew that if there was more that I could have done – if I could have practised something properly or prepared better – then that did me in. On the flipside, if we lost and I couldn't have delivered any more, it was still really hard but in a way I could cope.

I guess because of my own personal experience, when I hear about kids who want to be professional cricketers, footballers, boxers or whatever, I often feel concerned. The percentage is so small for success that it means at some point most kids have to deal with the fact that they're not good enough. It's brutal. I'm so fortunate that I've never had that conversation in my career and I don't know what it would have done to me if I had.

It does annoy me when people describe sports people's success as 'lucky'. For example, you'll have Wayne Rooney, or whoever it may be – 'He's lucky, him. Look at him, he earns all this money per week.' Well, nobody describes a doctor or a solicitor or an accountant as 'lucky' and they've only begun studying for that profession when they get to 17 or 18, starting formal training towards a degree. In sport, these lads and girls have started at six, seven or eight years old. An elite athlete might not be getting an academic qualification as such, it's not the same as going to university, but if you count the hours that they've worked to get there, that's more than good fortune. We could make the nature and nurture argument – nature can play a part in your genetics, if you have a particular physique – but after that, it's down to them. So, I have some sympathy with professional footballers and the dog's abuse they receive around the clock on social media and from the crowds in the stands.

When I'm working on talkSPORT, we will find ourselves discussing salaries that must seem utterly ridiculous to people. Whenever Paul Pogba, the Manchester United and France midfielder, gets a mention, it's always with his £300,000-per-week price tag. I bet he didn't get his ears pierced at Claire's

FAILURE AND SUCCESS

Accessories in Nottingham! It sounds daft, Pogba never gave himself that value, that's what was decided for him, the market dictates that. He's worth whatever a club is willing to pay for him, and that's where we are at. The money's there for the players, so why not take it? Who in their right mind would turn that down if it was the currency and going rate? Look how well Marcus Rashford has done with his wealth and I'm sure Pogba has been incredibly generous, too.

In the same vein, it's fine if you want to say I'm 'lucky' to host *Top Gear*, you are perfectly entitled to your opinion. I'm lucky in that it's great to have a job I love but what you don't see, and this extends to so many careers, is the graft behind the scenes. A lot less people saw the show I made where I traipsed around America jumping off cliffs and barely anyone watched my dodgy TV shows in the middle of the night or heard me doing Radio 5 Live graveyard shifts to get experience. I got my head kicked in on a daily basis learning to be a boxer for the sake of a documentary. So, it's not luck, it's pure hard work – that's what success boils down to in my book. It's a life lesson for me: application and hard work will take you a long way, much more than natural talent will if effort isn't applied. This is something I've learned the hard way.

He's already had plenty of mentions, but I'm really good mates with Rob Key, the former Kent and England cricketer and now the jewel of Sky Sports cricket. Over the years he's had more than his fair share of criticism but he covered all the Test matches through the night, really unforgiving hours. He worked his way up the hard way and took no shortcuts.

I can't say it more forcibly in this book: just give yourself the best chance possible to succeed. From my experience when I fail, I know I can live with it if I know I've done everything in my power, in my gift, to succeed. It's when I hadn't done that, I can't live with myself. One of the overriding feelings that I have about my cricket career is disappointment. In the early days, I didn't always give myself the best chance to succeed so I do sometimes lie awake at night contemplating that.

If you are an aspiring sportsman or woman, you will have days in your career when things go your way just by luck and raw talent, but if you go out expecting those moments, I can guarantee they won't happen for you. And I think I was guilty sometimes of thinking I could rely on that, that those moments would always come when I needed them and that may have contributed to me not being as dedicated as I should have been at times. And now I look back and wonder if my career would have been longer if I had. Though, having said that, there were times in my career when I played ridiculous cricket, when I had no right to, and just pulled it out of the bag . . .

I did it once when I got 100 in a dead game against South Africa. It was Michael Vaughan's first game as captain; Graeme Smith had got a double hundred and we were getting absolutely battered. The top four were out overnight going into the fourth day, so me and Steve Harmison had gone back to the hotel and told the rest of the lads we would be having 'a quick drink' at the bar.

We got a couple of pints of Stella at the Marriott in Regents Park. Two turned into three and that turned into four pints. On his way out for dinner, Vaughany asked us what our plans were for the evening. We told him we were planning to have a couple then an early night. Vaughany came back in about 1:30am, as he was out early in the day and his game was over, and we were about 13 pints of Stella down. Absolutely hammered. Stella does you, doesn't it?

Vaughany tried to give me a proper bollocking, which was the wrong time because I wasn't in the best of states. I was on the backfoot a bit, telling him, 'Woah, Vaughany. I tell you what, your game is over, MINE is not! Have a go at me tomorrow because I bet I get a hundred.'

Now, by that point in my England career, I had only ever scored a solitary hundred. I didn't believe it at all that I could get another one the following day, especially as the promise was slurring out of the mouth of a very drunk man. He said to me, deadpan, 'No, you won't.' So I asked him for odds and he went, 'Thousand to one.' I came straight back at him and said, 'Perfect, I'll have £100 on it.' Not a bad bet, even with the nick I was in.

So, Vaughany's gone off to bed and I went back to the bar and had a couple more with Harmy. We'd had 15 pints by this point.

When I got to the ground the next day, I was absolutely hanging. I was stinking of booze, sat on the balcony by the ledge with Jimmy Anderson next to me, looking horrified. He asked if I was alright and I said, 'Nah, I've got a couple of problems here. One, I'm minging. I'm stood here sweating in a total mess. And second, I've had a bet with Vaughany that I'm going to get a hundred, so I've got to get one.'

I went out and I just swung at everything, and I hit EVERY-THING. Me and Harmy put on 98 for the last wicket. Harmy got three and he was laughing at the other end. I was just swinging for fun.

Vaughany never paid up, of course, but it wasn't about the money. I got away with it and money can't buy that.

Mistakes

In professional sport, there is an expectation that you should know everything when you are 24 or 25. I often wonder if it's the same for musicians or other professions. The reality is, you make so many mistakes when you are young. Now I'm 43, I have the wisdom and maturity that would have allowed me to be so much better as a professional athlete.

When you are young and fearless and you have just found

your form, it's a magical moment in a sportsman or woman's career, I always think. I remember when Wayne Rooney first came on the scene for Everton and scored against Arsenal. He was amazing for club and country, you could sense the excitement every time the ball was anywhere near him.

I was the opposite of Rooney. He made a huge impression in his first appearance for Everton, for Manchester United and for England. I'm pretty sure he was brilliant in his first game for DC United, too. However, my debuts were bad. I've never been good at debuts – that has followed me into television and entertainment. I always take a bit of time to get it, but I don't think it's down to ability. For me, I think it's all about acceptance, just getting a bit more comfortable in my surroundings, and more importantly, with the people I'm working with.

When I played cricket and it didn't go well, it was always when I was putting too much emphasis and attention on my own game. I made performing at the highest level so important in my head that I tightened up and it affected me negatively. I don't seem to do that with TV. It sounds terrible, but it's not the be-all and end-all – that's what gives me the freedom to make it work. Often, I catch myself saying, 'If it all finished tomorrow, I wouldn't be bothered.' But deep down, I know it probably would bother me.

I look back at my cricket career, the one thing that really

screams louder the older you get is that crushing realisation that you don't get a second chance to replay it. It's so frustrating because it's such a waste of time going over all those things but I do it all the time. If I knew back then how to train, how to dedicate myself to looking after my body, of course I would have done it. I would have been so much better – but thoughts like these would do me in if I let them, I have to let it go and move on with my life.

When I look back, I wasn't responsible enough between 18 and 23, but the second half of my career was completely different. What I do regret is not getting more help with the mental demands of the game. I've learned the hard way that your head controls everything. You can spend hours in nets, batting and bowling, you can dedicate yourself to strength and conditioning, but if your head isn't right, you can't control any of it. You need to be tuned in and mentally sharp, which I wasn't, because we didn't categorise that as part of the training schedule as we should have done. I didn't know about depression, or how it would manifest itself in my performances. Now I do, and I could have learned so much from that.

These days, it's often just me on my own travelling for work. When I'm mulling my life over, I rarely give myself a pat on the back. It's the one thing that spurs me on. The constant inner monologue wondering, 'If I had done this, or if I had done that . . .' Though, on the flipside of that, no matter what I wanted to do, I don't think I would have been able to achieve that and be totally satisfied. It keeps me up at night – it actually keeps me hungry and moving forward.

The environment you're in, you become the product of. For that reason, I could barely watch *The Last Dance*, the Netflix documentary about Michael Jordan. I absolutely love the shoes, I've got loads of them, but the psychology of sport and winning was too much to re-live.

If I'm being brutally honest, I should have been the Michael Jordan of cricket. I should have been the one who was cutting a path for other players. In my head I wanted to be. I had all these visions about how I wanted to be, how I wanted to lead, how I wanted to perform, but I wasn't confident enough when I was younger to cope with the fallout of what that ambition and drive would have created. I ended up being led by the pack rather than leading them. I should have been calling people out, demanding more of them and more of myself, but I didn't do it because I wanted to please.

You only need to watch one episode of *The Last Dance* to realise Michael Jordan wouldn't have been the sporting icon he is if he had been a people pleaser. Friendship isn't always a recipe for success in the dressing room. Jordan was a ferocious competitor with an appetite and determination for victory that fortunately matched his talent. His attitude reminded me of the famous Sir Alex Ferguson quote: 'You only need four to carry your coffin.' In other words, you know who your friends are and you could probably count them on the fingers of one hand. If you want to please people and be best pals with your team-mates, there's a good chance it won't work.

I know that I wanted to conform. I wanted to be popular. I didn't, and still don't, like confrontation. I'll have it when it's necessary, don't get me wrong, but I didn't go looking for aggravation in an attempt to get more out of those players around me in the dressing room, or to get more out of myself.

I really kick myself about my career in cricket. I was decent and I think I could have done better. Then you throw in a few other things, like making myself sick after most meals, and it's actually a miracle that I did what I did. I was hungry a lot of the time, and that affected my mood, which must have affected my performance. No matter how much I think about it, it will never be enough for me. I look at my stats and my heart sinks and I hate being compared to other players based on those numbers. They don't really add up. But I was Man of the Series and Man of the Match so many times against the best teams in the world, and that's what matters to me because that shows England have probably won, and I have had the biggest influence on the game. With me, it was feast or famine – I was either the best or the villain of the piece.

I genuinely believe when you make a decision at any point

in time it's based on how you feel at that exact moment. When you look back with hindsight, you forget all the emotional attachment that came with it. You completely forget the situation and the reasons why you made that decision at that time.

Far too much drinking the night before the game? Choosing not to practise as hard as you could? Playing a bad shot at a bad time? Having a spectacular row with someone? All these questions seem really clear-cut with the benefit of hindsight. I look back at mistakes I made in my career and I think, *Why on earth did I do that?* But now I don't have all the shit that was going around in my head then that made me choose that option.

Talking about life lessons, one of the things I wish I'd done with my mental approach to the game when I was 16 is that when I was told to control the controllables, I wish I had listened. Even at 25, I still hadn't learned that. What happened much later is that the coaching I received was about attempting to turn your weaknesses into a strength. If you have the ability to genuinely and honestly acknowledge what you can't do, then you can do something about it. We had sports psychologists in the squad, but I saw them as a weakness back then, not a strength. For me it was almost a dirty word, used by weak people not mentally robust enough to cope. In fact, it was the opposite and that bravado was completely misplaced.

I didn't watch cricket for a while after I retired but I've come back to it and started enjoying it again as a fan. One thing I'm not as an ex player, and I've seen so many who are, is bitter about those players still in the game. I can enjoy other people's performances. Ben Stokes is brilliant – I can watch him when he does well and say 'bastard', but I do it with a grin.

You see how Cristiano Ronaldo goes about his business – a guy who will probably play at elite level into his forties because he has looked after himself impeccably. I read about Ronaldo, watch the Michael Jordan interviews and all I can surmise is, I could have done that. But I didn't, and I need to accept that.

As a result of that, I find that I'm now being too hard on my kids so they don't make the same mistakes as me. Rocky and Corey are doing well with their cricket, but I don't want them to suffer in the way I have with the feelings I endure now.

Over the last 18 months, when I was making the documentary about bulimia (*Living with Bulimia*, 2020), it stirred up a lot of emotions about my early career in cricket. We found some footage of me signing my first professional contract at Lancashire, but I'd forgotten about it.

Now I've had the chance to discuss my bulimia, I can say that it wasn't a bad performance considering I was chucking up in the toilets every day. I was suffering from depression; I just thought all the way through my playing days that there was something wrong with me. I would have loved to have been better, but in all honesty, I'm not sure I could have been.

You can never answer that question and that's what makes life interesting.

We've got to move on with life, keep going forward and not dwell on the past. Though I'm the best at giving that advice but the worst at listening to it. I've been lucky to find the equivalent mentors through the rest of my career. Seek out your David Lloyd, your Bumble, and you'll find your way.

What is Success?

I can't think of anything else other than cricket that would have given me the life I have now, but my agent Katie always says, you can't sit and wait for the phone to ring, you have to make things happen for yourself. At the same time, I think it's so important to stop and realise what we've actually got. Concentrate on that, not what you haven't got. Try living in the moment and not wishing life away, thinking about the future. I was incredibly guilty of that when I was younger and it didn't go well for me – you're always chasing and chasing, desperate to move on, or what you perceive to be 'up'.

I was asked recently if I had a five-year plan and my only answer was, my plan is to work as little as possible. What I've found is the more I do, the more work I tend to get. I can't unpick how that's working and I don't want to. I'm just going with it and seeing it through.

I wanted to work less, not feel the pressure to earn as much and have a quieter life, but then I landed *Top Gear* not long after that and as a result, my name appears to be linked to loads of other work. I shouldn't complain, I'm really enjoying it.

The problem with success is that everyone monetises it. We have these mad institutions like The Sunday Times Rich List, as if what you have in the bank is a true measure of success. In TV, you are judged by the shows you do and often, the awards.

Success for me should be judged by your family, friends and who is around you. How happy you are is dependent on that and it's something I'm always striving for. Earning money is all well and good, but I wouldn't swap any amount of money for my real friends. I would swap money for my kids to be happy, because their happiness is a true measure of success.

Money can buy you time with great holidays, but our measure is skewed by the world we live in. My mates with less complicated lives are in such a good place: they are happy with what they've got. And that's the ultimate success, being happy with what you've got.

Big Spender

When I was younger, I grew up with not very much in the way of possessions or material wealth. Then when I started earning decent money, I was reckless with it to the point that I was nearly declared bankrupt when I was 21.

FAILURE AND SUCCESS

I'm definitely not a financial advisor but I've learned an awful lot – and most of it the hard way. You can complicate things as much as you like, but the basic economics are so simple: if you spend more than you earn, it doesn't work out. I got sucked in, I took my eye off the ball and suddenly I couldn't pay the big bills landing on my doormat.

I've been in that position where debt seems insurmountable, like you can't claw your way out of a dark position. If there's one thing I can pass on is that you can rebuild your life and it's never too late.

I started earning half decent money after I played for England coming through county cricket. Rather than focusing on the sport, I got lost in everything off the field. I found myself in a position where I simply couldn't pay a tax bill so I had to borrow a significant amount of money to settle the debt. It meant I had to move out of my house at the time, move back in with my mum and dad and I was left with no other choice other than to screw the nut and sort myself out. I can completely understand why people go massively off the rails when they hide financial hardship, it can be a lonely, depressing place. That's one of the reasons I've taken jobs that I don't necessarily want to. If by me doing that job I don't particularly like gives my family a better life, then so be it. I can justify that to myself no problem. How many people can get out of bed in the morning and skip to work with a smile on their face? Look at what people do for a living: proper jobs, graft, a back-breaking shift of manual labour or spirit-crushing things to make ends meet.

I'm in such a fortunate position that I have to check myself for getting a bit precious when I'm on the cusp of turning down a job for a petty reason. I've found myself having a whinge-up about work and then I'll remind myself I'm being a prick. My agent Katie brings me back to earth with a bump if I get a bit carried away with myself. Tell you what Katie's brutal! Her uncle is John Lydon from The Sex Pistols and she makes him look shy and retiring. She's a lovely person but when it comes to telling you straight, there's no one quite like her.

We locked horns the other week about contract negotiations for a job. It was a good offer but it wasn't what we thought it was going to be and I was talking it through with her in detail. Suddenly, I found myself having that out-of-body experience; I could hear myself prattling on and I could see Katie's frown getting deeper. Richard, the head of the management company, was hiding and I knew what was coming my way. I was being ridiculous and she was spot on to point it out in the direct fashion she always does. She put the boot in and told me exactly where I was being a prick.

Later that day, I phoned her back to apologise because she was right.

You do get wrapped up in things.

CHAPTER SIX

FAME

'So we walked in and he's right there, Elton John. I love his music – I used to sell it in Woolworths.'

Hard, Fast and Short

One thing that drives me mad is famous people offering affirmations with all the 'follow your dreams, and do what makes you happy' claptrap. More often than not, it's advice offered from a place of success, wealth and comfort coming from people who don't have to worry about work or are completely loaded with cash. It's very easy to forget what it was like to get there, all the thankless stuff that you have to do and the moments when it feels like you're swimming against the tide.

Like taking a pedalo out to sea when you've had too much to drink, but let's not get back into that.

There's something ugly about the association with people doing what is perceived as a 'normal' job. Social media has definitely fed the desire to seek out fame and fortune, whereas holding down a good job and working hard was what used to command respect. You hear disparaging remarks about working in a supermarket, as if working in Tesco is the worst thing that you could ever do. It's out of order. My time on £3.77 at Woolies was as valuable a contract to me as the biggest fee I was paid by the ECB or for any telly job.

In my opinion, the fame that comes with success in sport is a horrible by-product. When I looked at athletes like Daley Thompson when I was growing up, I never saw it in the context of fame. I didn't look up to Mike Tyson, John Barnes, Ian Botham and Viv Richards because they were household names, I wanted to emulate their sporting achievements. I watched them and thought, *I want to be able to do what they do, I want to be brilliant at that.*

I can remember back to a few times in my career when it hit me that I was becoming famous. There was a book that came out every year called *The Cricketers' Who's Who* with every player's picture in it and a write up. At every ground there were autograph hunters and they would ask you to sign your picture in the book. It was mad when I started to get the odd person recognising me. Then when I first played for England the game changed and I could tell people were beginning to know who I was.

It was the fat stuff that really got me, though. That was the darker side of fame, if you want to call it that. That was the first time that it went large, for want of a better word. For anyone who doesn't know my story, I was a big lad when I was younger – mainly due to the alcohol, bad diet and being naïve.

It became a bit of a thing in the newspapers at the time, then it poured out of the crowds at games.

There was a real watershed moment when I topped the scales at over 19st and I thought they had to be broken. At one point I'd been 14st, then suddenly there was a swing of over 5st and I couldn't work out how it had happened. I took a long, hard look at myself and thought, *Shit, this is out of hand.*

Looking back, I wish someone had told me my weight was spiralling. It was during an England medical with our physio, a big Welsh lad called Dean Conway, when the alarm bells sounded. He used to call me 'Mungo' because I looked like the big lad off *Blazing Saddles*. He said, 'Fucking hell, Mungo, look at that! You're 128kg!' I was always used to doing everything in imperial measures, so the kilograms sounded huge, but over 19st was out of control at that point and I had to take action. From that point onwards, I made a concerted effort to change my attitude to drinking, eating and really focus on my fitness. I worked so closely with the physio and fitness staff, but kept it all behind closed doors. I wanted to preserve the myth that I was still out every night and not looking after myself, but the truth was, I was grafting really hard behind the scenes.

My career was taking off when I was in my early twenties and I got caught out with big drinking sessions making the papers. That brought a bit of notoriety and I suppose a little bit of interest. Then when I started performing at a high standard as well as being photographed coming out of a bar worse for wear, it was the perfect storm for coverage in the press.

Around that time I was done for drinking in the *Daily Mail*. I'd just done this big piece with a reporter about how I was turning my life around and I was losing weight. Then, straight after the interview, I went out in Manchester and managed to get photographed coming out of the Press Club at 4:30 in the morning, shit-faced. That was the first time I appeared in the front section of the paper. The fat stuff was making the middle pages and I'd be on the back as well, playing big Test matches. There just seemed to be quite a lot going on – including my ex-girlfriend selling her story.

I was in the dressing room during a Test match. I was playing in Birmingham and I had just met Rachael, my wife-to-be, for the first time the night before. I'd had a drink with her in the hotel and then turned up the next day for the game, the last day of the Test match against Sri Lanka. I was last man in the dressing room. All the lads had got a copy of the *News of the World* and they were laughing away to themselves.

'Who is it?' I asked.

'It's you, silly bollocks.'

Oh, fuck.

The headline read: 'FLINTOFF'S LOVE-MAKING LIKE HE'S BOWLING HARD, FAST . . . AND SHORT OF LENGTH!'

I had to go out and play and obviously I got annihilated.

The crowd had all read it too. They were shouting, 'Oh, fast and straight, eh?' 'Oi, tiny cock, here, want some Viagra?' I had to stand and take it.

Michael Vaughan was skipper. He didn't put me in the slips, the position I field everyday, did he? No, he put me on the boundary in front of everyone. I'd have done the same, though. That was how it worked at the time. I would have dished it out all day long if it was someone else.

The match finished and I took Rachael out for dinner that night. It was so awkward. We went out to the Living Room in Birmingham and sat down, ordered a bottle of wine and some food. We were just chatting away, still getting to know each other. I asked if she had seen any press, hoping she'd seen the nice piece about me in *The Times* that day rather than the *News of the World*'s critique! It turns out that she had read all of it, but it couldn't have been too bad. We had a laugh about it and despite being short of length we got married and had four kids, so it works.

Things really changed for me during 2005. Life was different after our Ashes triumph because it was all over the papers – front page, back page, middle pages. I did my best to shelter the family because during that series, in between Test matches, I went away on great holidays with them. It was only afterwards that I realised how big an achievement it was. England went bonkers for a bit, then it slowly died down.

In 2009, my last series, I remember the first and second Test match I got five wickets. After the second Test, I went to meet Piers Morgan. I'd arranged to have dinner with him on the last night of the Test. Irrespective of what happened, it was the date we set. It just so happened I had a good day, but I still wanted to go out with him. I was in the cab on the way to dinner and cars were pulling up alongside us and waving, with people beeping horns. Rachael said, 'It's happening again, isn't it?' I turned around and said, 'I fucking hope not! I can't put up with this again.'

We went to The Punchbowl Pub in Mayfair because Rupert, his brother, was running it. Guy Ritchie owned the pub and it got out of hand with the paps after I had my fish and chips. I must have had ten pints of Guinness, coupled with some bottles of red with Piers. He said, 'The paparazzi have turned up outside.' I said, 'Yeah, of course they have.'

There's a surprise, nobody knows we're here, we've got a lock-in but they've turned up.

He said, 'I've got this.' So, as we were leaving, he opened the door and he's in all the pictures, front and centre. It was funny seeing his face when they said, 'Fred's there, we don't want you.'

I actually had my worst experience with a photographer recently when I was down in Devon, just past Exeter, doing my first shoot for the clothing company, Regatta.

I was in this seaside resort doing some promo shots and we were filming outside a barber's. People were good as gold down there and so polite about asking for pictures and saying hello. I was sat outside and this pap popped his head in and started a chat about a mutual pal we had. He asked for some pictures and I said, 'that's fine, just give me five to ten minutes so I can get this shot,' but he started getting in the way of the official photographer.

He then started having a go, saying I'd changed as soon as we asked him not to get in the way. I was walking back to our base with Sara from my management and the rest of the team on the shoot and this guy started having a proper go, saying, 'You've turned into a fucking bellend these days, Flintoff. You're worse than Brad and Ange!' He kept calling me names and he was picking a fight. The lad started taking his top off and squaring up, but then I could see his mate was filming it all, waiting to get a reaction – I've never experienced anything like it.

Jeremy Beadle, John Major, Elton John and Michael Caine

I once shared a limousine with Jeremy Beadle. I think it was around 2007, I was going to a charity dinner at the Grosvenor House and a couple I know, who were staying in The Savoy, invited us to join them. They very kindly put me and Rachael up, which was a really nice touch. We were on their table for this plush dinner but decided we were going to have a drink at the hotel before we headed out.

We got into the bar and who's sat there? Only Jeremy Beadle with his missus! He's got a bottle of champagne on the go and a silk scarf around his neck.

I can be funny with famous people – put me in front of any footballer and I'm not arsed (apart from Barnsey, admittedly). If you put Jimi Hendrix there, no problem – 'You alright, Jimmy?' Former Arsenal and Manchester United striker Robin van Persie's kids were at the same school as mine and so were Wayne Rooney's, but when Les Dennis's kids started at the school, I was saying, 'Look at him, he's got a kid here. How good is this? It's Les Dennis! The actual Les Dennis. Seriously, THE Les Dennis!'

It was much the same with Jeremy Beadle. I kept saying, 'Rachael, that's Jeremy Beadle. That is Jeremy Beadle.' She couldn't understand why I was excited. I kept trying to get my face in his eyeline, hoping he'd see me and say hello. I was at the bar so in the end I just politely said, 'Hi, you alright?'

He replied straight away: 'Oh, Andrew. Such a pleasure, young man.' We got chatting and it came up in conversation that we were all going to the same event so I offered to get a cab, but Jeremy pipes up, 'No, I've got the limo outside. Come with us.' So, we had a bottle of champagne then decided to go in this white limo to the event. I was sat in a limousine drinking champagne with Jeremy Beadle so I made sure we asked the driver to go the long way so we could milk it as much as possible. I was pinching myself – the actual Jeremy Beadle! It felt like being in the presence of greatness. One of the most engaging, intelligent people, he talked to me about cricket but a lot of the time I just found myself looking at him. He was talking about TV, he was asking about me and where I came from. It was a brilliant experience. I'm so glad I had the chance to meet him before he died.

Jeremy was one of those people, if you'd told me when I was a kid that I would be in a car with him when I grew up, I wouldn't have believed you. He was like a mythical being when I was growing up. It's the same with Noel Edmonds – he was so famous, I would have been happy working as Mr Blobby's sidekick. In fact, at 19st you could have painted some yellow spots on me and I'd have looked the part!

The problem with TV now, and in the world, is that Beadle is *not* about, Noel doesn't have his house parties anymore and Barrymore can't find his hotspots. Les Dawson's not filling in the blanks and Bruce isn't playing his cards right, either. Now it's left to cricketers, ex-footballers and a bloke from Bolton called Paddy. It's not good game, it's game's gone!

I had the same Beadle vibes with former prime minister, John Major. Not because he was a comedy character, just realising the magnitude of the role he had in my life. Over the years I've met him a few times in passing, but we ended up on the balcony of The Oval a few years ago at a Test match against India and had a proper chinwag. I quite like the old school stuff within cricket. I'm not a traditionalist, but to me, going in the committee room is still a big thing. When I met John, it felt like that arena was his domain. He had a confidence I didn't expect – he was showing his human side. I felt like I was talking to a bloke called John, who was lovely and not a world leader. Mickey Stewart (former England captain Alec Stewart's dad) was also there and used to be my coach when I was aged 14 to 16 – I love Mickey!

You've got all these old boys who've been on the committee for years and I really enjoy it because I always learn something from them. I remember John Major having a drink with broadcaster Sir Trevor McDonald. We have the same agent, Thommo, so we often find ourselves in the same company. It's mad being at cricket, listening to these titans in conversation about foreign policy in the eighties and the countries they visited, the characters they met, all over a good drink.

I still find it surreal that I was sat watching cricket at The Oval and I was in deep conversation with John Major. This man was a prime minister. Think what you like about him, and whatever political party or whatever views you have, I'm sat with the PM! I'm from Preston and I'm sat there with John Major! Here's a fella who my nan used to write to. I've seen his replies from Number 10 Downing Street. Nan also used to write to the Queen and get letters back. She'd write, 'Andrew's gone to South Africa playing cricket and Christopher's doing this . . .' And you always got a reply back in those days.

I'm going to have to tell him, I thought. So I plucked up the courage and said, 'Funny one, John. My nan used to write to you when you were PM. I don't expect you to know and don't even wing it, but she always had a reply from the office and she was always over the moon. I'd like to thank whoever it was.'

He said, 'No, we used to get a lot of that and we always used to reply. It was important to do that.'

I ended up having a conversation with him about his family. He started telling me that his dad was a concert hall singer and, get this, his mum was a trapeze artist! Now, whether he's having me on here, I don't know, but I was believing every word of it. I'm sat there, enthralled, not talking about cricket, not about politics. John Major was telling me about his mum and dad! It was a similar thing with Jeremy Beadle. Take away the fame, the notoriety and the money, and they're just fascinating personalities.

It's funny, because I met David Cameron in 2010 when he was prime minister and it just wasn't the same. We went to

Number 11 for a dinner party after getting the big invitation. I didn't really know what I was going for. I was filming for Sport Relief and we were all running late so we turned up, me and the missus, in a bit of a panic. I'd been told Gary Barlow was going with his missus, but apparently Gary pulled out so his place was taken by James Corden and his wife, Jules.

We went into the kitchen and there's a dining table, which we all sat around, and it was fucking weird. He comes in, 'Call me Dave,' rolls his sleeves up, sits down. We had a glass or two of red but I didn't speak to Cameron all night.

He was a *Gavin & Stacey* superfan, so you can imagine James was loving life. There he is, the PM, quoting Smithy. You'd have thought James was the Prime Minister and he might as well have been for that night. I barely said a word and at one point, the missus was kicking me under the table because I'd got my head in my hands (sometimes I forget myself and she knows it). At this point, 'Dave' decided to tell a couple of Putin stories, which I reckon was his usual sportsman dinner material that he just rolls out.

We retired to the lounge for drinks and I'm sat on a pouf, he's on a couch and I'm just perched on this little thing with a whisky, looking massive. It was so uncomfortable listening to David Cameron waffle on. Then, at about 10pm, he says, 'Right, got a busy day tomorrow, we've all got to go.'

We called it a night and I never heard from him again.

FAME

I had dinner with Archbishop Desmond Tutu in 2004. What a man he is! It was in South Africa and we met through Sir Elton John, who has become a friend over the years.

He's a great man, Elton. I love him. The kids do as well, they listen to all his music and that's so nice because it's just a different world now when it comes to fame and talent, though young people have some great people to look up to now. I might have had Daley Thompson but they have Man U's Marcus Rashford, who has turned out to be a saint.

The first time I met Elton was when we were attending this function at a winery in South Africa when I was playing out there in 2004. It was one of the first nights out we'd had because the baby was with us, Holly. So, Mum and Dad looked after her and off we went. We didn't know what we were going to, but had the black tie on. Fucking hell! We turned up at this winery and it was beyond beautiful – it was one of Elton's White Tie and Tiara dos.

So, we walked in and he's right there, Elton John. I love his music – I used to sell it in Woolworths. We had a look for the table plan and realised we were sat on a table next to Desmond Tutu. To make it even weirder, Lee Ryan from Blue was there too. I was thinking, *Is Beadle about?* It was off-the-scale in terms of how ridiculous it was.

So, we got to the table and Desmond Tutu rolled into town. And he was just the life and soul of this table all night long. So, there we were, sat on a table with Desmond Tutu, the Archbishop, Lee Ryan and Elton John.

Elton was doing his bit on the piano and Lee Ryan joined in with 'Your Song', while I was just chatting to Desmond Tutu and he's a gag a minute. He's got this infectious laugh.

It was bonkers.

I might have some type of Rain Man tendencies or something because I learn songs and I love them and I know lyrics to so many of them. And I've always loved Elton John songs. It was 'Rocket Man' for me. During The Ashes in 2005, I used to play it in the dressing room. I was one of the main players in the team, so I could put on what I wanted and if anybody put anything else on, it would be taken straight off. Everybody in the dressing room got into it and it became an anthem for 2005. Bizarrely, you put it on in the dressing room and it just seems to settle everyone – it certainly worked with me. We were doing well and the song reminded us all of success. It was subliminal, but looking back, it worked. It got out in the press and I received a signed CD sent from Sir Elton John.

So, in my testimonial year, 2006, I thought, *I'll chance my arm and ask him to perform.* I asked if he'd do a function for me and straight away, he said yes. The event was at Battersea Park. He brought a piano, sang at the dinner (did ten songs) and then I got up on stage with him and murdered 'Rocket Man'. I was so nervous, I couldn't even open my mouth. He didn't sit for the dinner because Watford were playing, he watched the game in his Winnebago instead. Once the football finished and he joined us, I was chatting to him and once you got past the fact it was Elton John, it was staggering to hear his knowledge of sport. In fact, his general knowledge was unreal. The night was incredible. I was pinching myself. To think this young lad from Preston, who played a little bit of cricket, has got one of the biggest musical stars in the world performing at his testimonial dinner. For that, I will always be thankful to the great man, Sir Elton John.

The following year, I bought a couple of tickets to his White Tie and Tiara event. I walked in with Redknapp, who I didn't really know then, and Frank Lampard, who was lovely. I found myself chatting away to Sir Michael Caine and Sir Tom Jones. As you do at these functions, you have to go over to the big board to find out where you are sitting. I thought I would be sat at the back somewhere, possibly with Redknapp. Instead, Sir Elton John had put me on his table with Bernie Taupin as well. It was such a huge privilege.

It was the second time I had met Michael Caine; the first was at The Ivy. I had gone for dinner with Rachael during a Test match. We must have been doing well as we had a great seat. We were sat at the table, the next thing, I've looked up and Michael Caine is stood at the end of it.

'Hello, young man,' he said.

I replied, 'Hi, Mr Caine. Nice to meet you, I'm Fred.'

He said, 'I like what you do.'

I said, 'Oh, right. Thanks.' I was panicking, with zero chat for him. My missus was kicking me as if to say, 'Speak!' So I said, 'Oh, if you fancy, we're playing tomorrow at Lord's, I can get you tickets? At a stretch, I can get you lunch and tea vouchers as well.'

And he said, 'That's very kind of you but I only watch on television. Goodnight.'

Fucking hell! I was over the moon because he came to see us.

Fred the Celebrity Interviewer

I've been so lucky that my job has meant I've met some pretty special famous people. But I still have an uncomfortable relationship with the bizarre notion of fame and particularly 'celebrity' and I think that's because a lot of famous people wind me up.

I remember being a guest on Jonathan Ross's show, listening to the pop star Jason Derulo talking utter bollocks. What a whopper he was! He started moaning because his Nando's didn't turn up. I was sat on the end of the couch with Josh Widdicombe and Alex Brooker from *The Last Leg*. We were giggling like naughty kids, nudging each other every time Jason tried to tell us this extravagant story of his fancy house. It sounded like he lived at a Sea Life Centre! All I can remember is him boasting about having sharks, like he was some kind of shit Bond villain.

It bit me on the arse slightly though because the following day I found myself on a flight to LA to interview a series of Hollywood stars. It might be an inverse snobbery about celebrity, but it felt like someone was sending me a message.

I got the gig because I've been very lucky to have a big audience who seem to like me in Australia. It's like a trade-off with me and Shane Warne. He's welcome in the UK and I've been accepted on his home turf. My agent Katie negotiated some great deals for me to host some TV shows in Australia and it has given me lots of experience which has definitely helped me develop in TV back home. One of the gigs was doing celeb interviews, which then opened the door for me to go to LA in 2015 to interview Will Smith and Margot Robbie for the film they were releasing, *Focus*.

I got on the flight, went over to LA and I have to admit, I didn't have a clue what was happening. Once I'd dropped my stuff at the hotel, I was taken by coach to see the film and it wasn't good. I was jet-lagged and I'd be lying if I said I got through it all – I woke up in the theatre as the end credits were rolling and people were shuffling out. The next morning, I started to get my act together, thinking about what I was going to ask Will and Margot. I had all these suggested questions from the network, which were dreadful. So, I got a hotel menu from the restaurant and started scribbling down my questions in the gaps around the club sandwich options.

I didn't know I was in a junket. If you're unfamiliar with the term, that's a series of actors holed up in hotel rooms waiting to be interviewed in short appointments over the spell of a week by national and international journalists. It must be awful for them. I didn't even know what a junket was at that point, I just thought I was there to see Will and Margot on my own. It was pure *Notting Hill* awkwardness, when Hugh Grant pretends he's working for *Horse & Hound*. I was told by a publicist I would have to interview every single member of the ensemble cast, which was a pretty low point for journalism, and I started to panic.

Eventually I sat down and joined the queue. There was a girl there, one of Jack Whitehall's mates, so I asked her for some ideas. She started laughing about writing questions on the menu, so I binned it.

I could see a door with the name 'Gerald' written on it and I was thinking, *Who the fuck is Gerald? Who is he?* So, I got out my phone to frantically Google him but exactly as I connected to the hotel Wi-Fi, I was summoned for my chat with 'Gerald'.

The publicist said, 'Oh, lucky for you, you don't just have four minutes. You've got eight minutes, you've got double time!'

FAME

Four minutes too many. I walked in and a vaguely familiar, older gentleman called Gerald was sat in front of me. I recognised him from a Western, or some kind of cowboy film. He seemed like a lovely fellow. The Preston lad in me kicked into action and I managed to read the situation to find some kind of inspiration to make the chat work. Gerry had trousers with pockets on them coupled with a checked shirt – the kind of look that said he was an outdoorsy kind of guy. So out of nowhere, I heard myself asking my first question ever at a junket: 'Do you like fishing?'

His eyes lit up. He goes, 'Yeah, I love it. It's all I want to do.'

I was right in there. I could hear myself asking if he was a fly fisherman or whether he preferred sea fishing and he started telling me about the biggest fish he'd caught, going into a rant for about five minutes about how all the world leaders should just go on the side of a bank, fly fish and sort out all their problems.

Sorted. Job done. I got some good stuff from Gerry over the eight minutes, which became ten, because he was enjoying himself. I was walking out the door as he was inviting me fishing: 'See you later, G-Man!'

Then I was onto the next meeting. I walked in and, again, I didn't have the foggiest who this fella was. And he was a big fella. I'd seen him a bit in the film – he played the comedy role – and the three seconds of Googling the movie informed me it's about deception and conmen, which was beginning to feel pretty close to home for me as a Hollywood reporter. So, I thought I'd start with something challenging: 'When do you think it's alright to lie? When do you think it's OK to be deceitful?'

He came straight back and said, 'Well, I could call you an idiot. Would you know if I'm lying or not?'

The Preston in me came straight out again. Fifteen years of sledging at all levels had prepared me for this. I replied with a grin, 'Excuse me?'

He's fired right back, 'Well, I could say you're a moron. Would you know if I'm lying or not?'

Before it sunk in, I said, 'Do you know what, mate? I don't care, but if you want this interview to go this way, I'll start throwing some shit right back at you. Right?'

He said, 'No.'

By the end, though, we were having a laugh, even though it started a bit frosty.

After some mixed fortunes with Gerry and the big lad, I then had Margot and Will waiting for me. I was sat outside the room and everybody was pacing around looking nervous. As I went through, the room was in meltdown because the girl before me had tried to sneak a selfie and was getting bundled out as fast as possible. As I walked in, I spotted a draped velvet curtain. I thought it was a curtain you were supposed to appear through, like some sort of *Stars in Their Eyes* drama, so I started pushing at it. Not only did I push the whole fucking set down, I was then just stood there in front of two huge Hollywood stars like a total melon, saying, 'Arright,' like an extra in Brian Potter's talent show on *Phoenix Nights*.

An army of film people got things sorted in a flash and I sat down to get chatting. I started speaking to Margot Robbie, saying, 'You've worked with a lot of big actors in this industry, haven't you?' She was looking a bit nervous, expecting some tabloid question. I said, 'You've worked with Harold Bishop, you've worked with Madge. You didn't get Helen Daniels and Joe Mangle in your era, though?'

Margot started having a bit of a giggle and Will was going, 'Hey, man, what about me? What about me?' Margot was laughing because I was like, 'I'll get to you in a minute, Will.' I somehow then got the conversation onto Australian cricketers and hair transplants.

We were having an in-depth chat about Shane Warne's barnet and Ricky Ponting's treatment and Will jumped in with, 'Well, not a problem for me. Black don't crack, man.'

So, I found myself asking Will Smith if he would have a hair transplant and he started patting his head frantically, saying, 'Hey, man, I've been tested. This ain't going nowhere. I've been tested.'

I asked him why he'd been tested. What on earth would

you get tested for? And then at that point, the publicist started telling me to get back on track and so I told her I'd got some gold dust for Aussie TV, got up, said thanks and left.

I was secretly hoping that would be that with my junket interview career. Sadly though, after that one went reasonably well, I was wheeled out to interview Mark Wahlberg.

It didn't go well.

It was during the promo cycle for the film *Ted 2* (2015). It was absolute rubbish and the first one was rubbish as well. When I was checking in, I was chatting to some of the publicity team and I asked the usual questions about Wahlberg to see if I could glean some information for our chat. One of the publicists said, 'He's had a month of these interviews, so his patience is starting to wear a little thin.' For some reason I thought I'd be the one to turn it around and get the best out of him. How wrong I was. Having been on the other side of it now, I realise he might just have been sick of hearing the same question over and over.

I got a list of questions from the network but I didn't want to go down that route. So I sent Piers Morgan a text because he claimed, as he always does with famous people, that he was mates with him. He came straight back and said, 'Oh, he's a big cricket fan. He's involved in the Caribbean Premier League and all that.' So, the pressure was off, I thought I was in. But no, I got absolutely nothing. I would say 'not a sausage' but I think burgers are more his thing – I didn't get a Wahlburger.

We had eight minutes together. I dried up after two and even the stuff the studio gave me to ask fell on disinterested ears. To be fair, my questions weren't all that. I ended up saying, 'Is there anything you want to tell me about this film?' He just went, 'I'm done.'

I still had about three minutes to endure with him so I just said, 'No one's enjoying this, are they? Let's just not bother with it.'

So, I left Mark Wahlberg, hopefully for the last time for both of us, thinking it was finally the end of my career as a film reporter. It wasn't entirely bad though, because that experience made me think about how I behave with interviewers – you have to be understanding and realise it might be your 100th, but it's their first chat that day.

I also had to interview comedian and actor Seth MacFarlane, who was the voice of Ted – I thought I was going to see Seth Rogen from *Knocked Up*! I walked in and I didn't need the interview, so it was all a bit embarrassing again, but what a man he was, what a brilliant guy! I just had a chat with him that happened to be filmed. He couldn't have been more entertaining and engaging – full of mischief and personality.

My last chat was with the actress Amanda Seyfried and I'd been on Jonathan Ross with her.

So, I thought she might remember me, that I was on safe ground, that this was going to be an easy chat, but as soon as I walked in I realised she had no idea who I was, so I quickly resorted to the questions I'd been given by the network. The sound man I knew later told me it was possibly the worst interview he has seen anyone do! I've got the list of suggested questions. On this card, written down for me, it said Amanda's nickname was Gollum, after the character in *The Lord of The Rings*, so I asked her about that. She just looked at me with a death stare. It was written down, I showed it to her. I knew immediately someone was on the wind-up and I'd just insulted this poor girl. Someone had stitched me up – it was awful. I felt terrible offending her. I still think about it now. It makes my teeth itch to this day. I'm genuinely gutted. What a prick.

Not long after this debacle, I was asked if I wanted to interview Harrison Ford and so I had to come out of retirement.

When I got there a few seasoned Aussie journalists were pacing the halls, nervous about their big moment. One of them asked what I planned to talk to him about and I said, 'I'll just talk about *Star Wars*, I think, because it's coming back and he's in it again.' Another one asked if I was nervous, but it was more of an out-of-body experience because he was one of my heroes growing up. I don't get nervous, but this was as close as I had been.

Star Wars, Indiana Jones, The Fugitive, Regarding Henry,

Witness, *Patriot Games* and *Blade Runner* – all incredible films. Then, all of a sudden, he's sat there in front of me with big windows behind him overlooking Sydney Harbour Bridge. It was this perfect scene and I had a moment where I just thought, *How on earth have I got here?*

It was a long way from Woolies in Preston.

The cameraman did me a massive turn by recognising me and saying hello. It just so happened that this guy was a massive cricket fan, so I immediately caught Harrison's attention with this lad's sudden interest after a dull morning of chat. I knew he was involved in the Hollywood Ashes and the cameraman teed up the conversation perfectly.

I couldn't believe it when Harrison Ford piped up with the line, 'Oh, I know one of your mates. I worked with a really good mate of yours, Jack Whitehall?'

Jack had been a guest on Graham Norton's show when they first met on air. They'd got on so well, Harrison had come over to the table at Little House in Mayfair where Jack was having dinner with David Beckham, and gave Jack a hug!

I opened up with something like, '1977 was the year I was born and *Star Wars* came out. Never did I think I would be sat here talking to you. Did you think you'd be pushing a new *Star Wars* film now?'

We had a great laugh. I asked him how old Chewbacca was and he didn't know. Then I asked who he'd sooner be in real life – Han Solo or Indiana Jones – and he couldn't choose. It was a lovely interview so it felt like a far more appropriate way to bow out of my career as a film reporter.

I took a lot from that experience. I'm in a fortunate position where I can be bold with stuff, but I genuinely believe there comes a point where it's the right thing to walk out of a bad situation. I'm sure if I was younger and it was my first career, I would have endured the full eight minutes of Wahlberg, but hopefully someone reading this will take courage from it and when a line is crossed or the energy is wrong, they will call it out or walk away from the aggro.

Life is not a rehearsal.

The *Hello!* Debacle

I've made some terrible mistakes when I've been on the other side of an interview and the subject of the piece. Especially in the glossy magazine department, and I'm not talking top shelf, I'm talking about *Hello!*. Rachael and I did a magazine shoot in 2005 and I can only describe it as awful.

They offered a good bit of money and, being brutally honest, it turned my head. I was also convinced by my agent at the time that if I did this one thing, I wouldn't then have to do all the other interview requests. It didn't work out that way though, did it? The floodgates opened afterwards and we're still being offered stuff today.

Talk about pouring fuel on the fire. First of all, it wasn't done in our house because I wouldn't let them do it there, so they rented this other place. Oddly enough, I went to view it the other week and it has changed for the better. Back then, I was walking through the place shuddering.

I'd done photo shoots for cricket and loads of sponsorship stuff but never dipped my toe in entertainment. When I arrived, I could see a rail of clothes laid out for me. My missus still cringes to this day about how northern and forthright I was, saying, 'What are these clothes for? I've got my own clothes in my bag.'

So, I was taking off my clothes, not even in my own house, and they decided that I should put a dinner suit on. I was in full tuxedo when they broke the news that we'd be shooting in the kitchen. When I looked around, I could see the oven with all the cameras pointing towards it. The photographer started explaining how good it would look if I slipped a pair of oven gloves on and then pulled some pies out of the oven. So, I was standing there, bemused, saying, 'Are you winding me up? That is not happening. Just take your pictures.'

Looking back, I can't blame the people at *Hello!*. They were just trying to do their job, something which I had agreed to do. But I had a quick realisation that this wasn't the world I wanted to be in at that time. I just wanted to be a cricketer. Play for England, play for Lancashire and perform. I felt like a fish out of water. The insecurities all came back. There were no familiarities – the one thing that I enjoy, I like and I need. I wasn't in my house, I wasn't in my clothes, there were cameras around, and people I didn't know. Not an environment which I thrived in.

The *Hello!* situation was a strange one, but not long after, we got offered to sell our wedding. I weighed it up, then thought, *Actually, this is probably one of the few days of my life I'm not trying to make money*. I was hoping it was going to be a good investment, I wasn't trying to cover my losses at the start.

John Terry, former Chelsea and England captain, cracked me up. We lived around the corner from him in Cobham, Surrey, and we got on well. You hear loads of stuff about John but the older I've got, the more I've learned to take people at face value because I know some of the shit that's been said about me that isn't true.

We had kids in the same class at school. I always admired him, even amid the controversy, because even when there were things bubbling in the press about him he'd be straight in the schoolyard, fronting it out. If he had a bad game or there had been a bit of scandal, he'd be stood in the schoolyard in his Ugg boots. I felt like tipping my cap to him. We would always have a chat, he's good as gold.

I was at a football match once when our kids were playing and we were sat on a bench together. He got onto weddings and he's going, 'Did you sell your wedding, Fred?'

I said, 'No, I didn't, John. We had it in London in a place called Pavilion Road just because once you're in, there's no coming out. Nobody could get to us, no pictures.'

I asked him the same question and he said, 'Yeah, yeah. What happened was we sent a guest list and then they put a price next to the guests. That's how you earn your money, who they're going to get a picture of.' Then, with a massive grin on his face, he said, 'Fuck, if I'd have known you then, I'd have got eight grand for you!'

I may be very glad I didn't let the gossip mags in to take pictures of the wedding, but I will always regret that we didn't get it filmed. I really wish I could look back on it and see everyone there having a good time. That's definitely been a life lesson – there might be far too many camera phones now but there are still some moments worth recording.

We had former Rolling Stone Bill Wyman and his Rhythm Kings playing at the wedding! I played cricket with him, opened the batting for The Bunbury's. He used to bat with a fag in his mouth. So, we got chatting and I asked him to play at our wedding. He agreed as long as I squared up his band; he did it for free.

I had Georgie Fame on keyboard, Bill Wyman singing. The bizarre thing was, I was expecting him to get more of a reaction, but my mates just headed straight to the free bar.

Good Game, Good Game!

It still blows my mind that the level of fame I experienced completely changed when I did a Morrisons advert. It was a nice little earner until I lost the job to Ant & Dec. Morrisons decided to go 2-4-1 on that deal.

I had an embarrassing moment on the Morrisons' Christmas ad with Bruce Forsyth. We put up a Christmas market in Kingston, Surrey, in September so they could film and have the ad ready for TV by the end of November. It was right in the middle of a heatwave and we were all dressed up in hats and scarves as if it was mid-winter. They had to keep dabbing me down on set, I was so sweaty, it was torture.

The director was the same guy who did all the ads with Gary Lineker for Walkers Crisps. He asked me what I thought a director looked like, then pointed to himself and said, 'This is what a good director looks like!' He had a baseball cap and a jacket on. Then he told me, 'Stick with me and you'll be doing these for life!' I'd already done four by that point and got binned off during his reign.

So, we did the Christmas market bit and the whole premise was 'build it and they will come'. It was quite sweet, they had a couple of kids helping me, there was a Ferris wheel erected for the shoot. We moved into the studio to do some more filming and I was above Bruce on the Ferris wheel with the kids and he was down below, two girls draped around him. Apparently, he wouldn't leave his house in Surrey before 9:30am or stay later than 3:30pm, which you can only admire him for.

It was brilliant, he earned that so he made the rules.

He came on set to see me before we got started and first thing he said was, 'Hello, Fred, nice to see you. How's young Sam getting on?'

I couldn't believe it. When Darren Gough was taking part in *Strictly* I'd managed to get in to see him and asked Bruce for an autograph for a friend's son who was off to college to be a dancer. And he remembered! I was so impressed. He was mustard, a class act.

The last shot we had to do was me on the Ferris wheel above Bruce. He had to deliver the line, 'Freddie, this game pie is delicious!' and I had to say, 'Good game, good game, Bruce!'

The floor manager came in and told me I needed to give my line a bit more 'Brucie' – a Brucie bonus, if you will. He said to really ham up the 'good game, good game' line as if I was presenting *The Generation Game*. He assured me Brucie was fine with it and encouraged me to really let go. So reluctantly, and nervously, I agreed.

Next time round, I've fully committed. Full steam ahead with an over-the-top, chin-sticking-out, nose-wrinkling 'GOOD GAME, GOOD GAME!'

Brucie just looked at me, horrified. The girls looked disgusted. I cast an eye across to the crew and everyone's shoulders were going up and down – the camera lads were in fits of giggles. They had stitched me up like a kipper.

So Brucie came in and behaved like an absolute class act to me, a proper gentleman. I reciprocated by behaving like a class clown, a complete idiot, and I insulted a great man. Part of me wanted to congratulate the floor manager for the audacity of his wind-up. I tried to apologise to Bruce, to explain what happened, but it was coming up to half three and he wanted out. After my behaviour, he wanted out even more quickly. I was mortified. He must have been in the car going home, thinking, *The cheeky prick, getting me to sign Sam's autograph and behaving like that. Who does that Flintoff lad think he is?*

I just hope he could see that I'd been done. I couldn't get angry about it because coming from the dressing room culture, it was a good one.

The sad thing is I never saw Bruce again.

Memorabilia

The TV shows I make often give a big glimpse into my personal life. It took a lot for me to open up about bulimia, depression and drinking in 2019 but I put it out there because I've considered it at length and hoped that it might help someone suffering from the same problems as me, but there is actually a lot of stuff I just want for myself. We've got shoe boxes of pictures of us as kids and teenagers at my mum and dad's and I'm glad they're not online anywhere because they belong to us as a family. It's bad enough that the *ALOTO* boys got hold of the picture of me in my buggy. If you haven't seen it, there's a picture of me in a buggy when I'm about 18 months old. The lads have gone to great lengths to use it as a stick to beat me with because I look like Sloth from *The Goonies* in it.

It was funny for a bit, but it's gone too far now. It's become the laziest joke ever and my mum actually quite likes that photograph of me. I can't imagine what the other ones are like if she thinks that's a good one!

I'm under pressure at the moment because we're buying a new house and among all the clothes, we've found loads of memorabilia we've accumulated over the years – things like my England caps. The missus has always been at me to put them up on show somewhere, but I can't bring myself to do it.

There are two or three things that I cherish from my career. One's my first Lancashire cap, when I was nine, the other is my first bat and I have the first ever Compton-Miller medal, which was presented to me after The Ashes in 2005 for being the player of the series. For the rest of it, I'd just feel a bit self-indulgent, walking around the house surrounded by pictures of me. The BBC Sports Personality trophies are different because it's not even the fact that I won them. They're not pride of place, just on a shelf. The reason I like them is because they look so beautiful. I must admit though, I sometimes sit and look at them, because I remember as a kid that was the biggest night of the year, seeing all these sports stars that I admired, and now I've got two trophies on my shelf. How on earth has that happened?

I'd consider putting up a Shane Warne strip, or perhaps Keysey because he's a proper mate, but why would I hang a Glenn McGrath shirt up? I've got one but he just used to swear at me all the time. Why do I want to remember that? Also, when people come to your house, I would find it so embarrassing – walking past shirts and pictures of me playing cricket. It's just not what I'm about. The other, and possibly the main reason too, I still want to be a cricketer. I couldn't walk past shirts and pictures of me playing a game that I'm still wanting to play. It would be too sad. Who would want to live in a house, full of reminders of something you desperately want to do but you can't do it anymore? Not me.

On the flip side, what example is that setting to my kids? I want them to be proud of their performances. I want them to feel they could show them off, so possibly this is more about me and how I do things than anything else.

I loved winning at the time but I don't need to bask in it

FAME

after. So, for me, whether it's sport, awards, playing a game of table tennis or playing a sport now, I love the act of doing it. That point when you win is amazing but afterwards is awful – the adulation and attention isn't for me or the fawning or sycophancy, I just want it to stop afterwards. We can all go and celebrate or we can do what we want, but I struggle being given anything.

The treat was actually playing. Being in the position to play was reward enough for me, it wasn't about adulation afterwards, it was about the moment itself. Being awarded an MBE in the New Year Honours List of 2006 was nice, but I don't need that. Anyway, I think there are better things I've done in my life to get an MBE than play cricket. When we won and we would get the accolades and the attention, I hated that – I found it so awkward and embarrassing.

The podcast I recorded with Matthew Syed and Robbie Savage in 2017 was a bit ahead of the game. We won Audio and Radio Industry Awards and I picked up Best Newcomer. In total, we won three awards, but it was the same feeling all over again. Sav was loving it, but it wasn't for me. Don't get me wrong, it was a decent podcast and I thought we should have won but doing it, making it, that was reward enough. On reflection, I should have stayed at home that night.

For me, your house should always be a safe haven. Outside, you're that person everybody wants you to be or thinks you are. At home, I'm not famous and I love that so I don't need to hang stuff on the wall. But I think there's another reason I've never put anything up and it's because I don't want to see the relics of the past. It would be nice to be able to put a shirt up in my house one day. The problem for me is that it's a reminder of something that I still really want to do. It's also a reminder that I didn't do what I wanted to do, I didn't achieve what I think I could have.

A Viking Abroad

I see people round where I live, incredibly wealthy people, successful business people, and they are always after more. How much more do you want? I found out some of these wealthy people really want to be famous, that's their goal in life, which I don't get. I think they're mad – I don't want to be famous, I'd like a bit of money to be comfortable with the family and just fitting into the background. Would I like to be fully anonymous again? Yeah, to a point. But actually, I would be glossing over that it does work for me sometimes, like getting into a good restaurant!

Back in 2007, I was injured and I was getting a real kicking in the press for the World Cup and the 5–0 defeat in The Ashes over in Australia. The coach hammered me. Duncan Fletcher had just given me all the blame. I took it on my shoulders as I've always done when things go wrong, though I felt like he took a fucking liberty over that because it wasn't all my fault. As a result, I was in a bad place.

I went on a warm weather training camp to Florida, so I took the family with me to have a bit of a reset. I think they wanted me out the way, too. I found I really enjoyed no one recognising me there, no doubt partly because of everything that had been going on at home. I bought a load of American stuff so I was walking about wearing a basketball top and looking a bit of a dick. Clearly an Englishman abroad, or maybe a Viking abroad. Because I'm tall, I suppose that's why people would come up and ask, 'Are you a basketballer?' When I explained, they couldn't grasp what cricket was, confusing it with croquet.

While we were there, the pound was two-to-one on the dollar, which was unreal. We were renting a house on a golf resort and absolutely nobody knew who I was. We just went about, having a lovely time, and I said to the missus at one point, 'You know what? We could just cash it all in now, we could buy a café or a restaurant and start again.'

So, we seriously contemplated emigrating. We stayed there for ten weeks and then Rachael persuaded me that it wasn't really what I wanted to do with my life. She said, 'Really? You're going to stay here and run a café? You don't want to play cricket again for England? You don't want to put straight all the things that have gone wrong in the past two years? You don't want that opportunity?' Of course she was right and we came home. It's really interesting looking back at that time because I can understand the instinct to up sticks and start over again when you're taking a pummelling like I was. The fresh start always seems really tempting, but I genuinely believe running away doesn't solve your problems. It wouldn't have given me closure and I think I could have become quite bitter and stewed over it, had I just run away.

Nowadays everyone has a camera on their phone. I'm just so pleased that I didn't play cricket when all that was about. You could definitely move about more and enjoy a bit more of a life. Now I understand why sports people are guarded, where they don't say owt. Everyone's always after something. The picture culture's strange because you very rarely say no. It often happens at the worst possible moment – no one knows what you're talking about or what's going on at that precise moment. It's not a life lesson, but maybe read the room, get a sense of what you might be interrupting and if you get a bad vibe, think hard before you pose the big question about asking for a photograph.

I had a situation the other day at home that I felt bad about. On reflection, though, I think I did the right thing. I was getting out of my car after pulling up at the gates at home, and two Scouse lads were at my gates, waiting. They had a pile of blank cards to get signed and I've since heard they wait around town for footballers, then follow them home to ask for signatures.

It's like an organisation. They came at me like, 'Fred, will you sign these for us?' I said, 'Lads, I'm at home. Not now, sorry.'

But one of the lads was insistent: 'We know, we saw you at the petrol station and we followed you home.'

'What? You followed me home?' I said.

They went, 'Yeah.'

I wasn't having it. I feared that if I helped them out, they might come back again, so I needed to put a marker down and tell them it wasn't right. When I got in the house, I felt like a total prick, but it freaked me out a bit at the time. I'm sure it'll be going around their group of pals that I was the dick who said no – the stuff was probably just going straight on eBay anyway.

I don't ask for many pictures with people, but one that I can remember is Mike Tyson. At the other end of the showbiz spectrum, in 2016, I hosted the Mind Media Awards and the charity as a thank you got me a video message from Honey G! It was so funny. Honey G was on *The X Factor* and she became a bit of a guilty pleasure – that, and she does look like my mate, Rob Key.

I've been getting video messages for the kids, but I spent a while plucking up the courage to ask in the right way. For Corey's birthday, we got him a John Barnes retro England shirt – the one that Jay wears in *The Inbetweeners*, the red away kit. Ten minutes later, courtesy of Jamie Redknapp, the video drops on his phone, 'Hello Corey, this is John Barnes. You're 15 – happy birthday.' John Barnes, what a man.

I like watching Gordon Ramsay on telly but Rocky loves him. My son is really into cooking so I sent a message to Gordon and he sent a minute-and-a-half-long message for Rocky. He was so chuffed with it, so I understand the appeal.

I get asked a lot to record messages for birthdays or special occasions. One of the most common requests is to help with a best man's speech and I feel a strange pressure to help. Celebrity video company Cameo is actually a clever business where there is a price attached to a celebrity greeting or message. The business has been valued well over a billion dollars now. There are some big names on there and why not? It makes perfect sense if you command a fee and it doesn't sit badly with you, go for it!

I had a look on there and there was some folk asking for £6.50 who you haven't heard from in ages. Higher up the price scales is Barry from *EastEnders*, I'd like a message from him. Shaun is one of the best blokes ever. But the jury is still out for me on this. It doesn't matter if someone wants to pay £50 for it, why are we bothered? £250 for The Hoff? You used to drive Kit, you don't need to be on Cameo, you're Michael Knight, man!

The thing is, fame is such a fickle thing. Harrison Ford's entire life has been in the public eye because he's brilliant at

FAME

what he does, but you can tell he doesn't want the attention or the praise: he just wants to do his job. I'm sure he would say the same thing – don't go looking for fame or money because you won't find happiness. Find the reward in doing something you love.

I've just finished the chapter doing exactly what I dislike – offering some mad celebrity affirmation. See? That's what a bit of notoriety does to you.

CHAPTER SEVEN

MONEY

'It was all a bit Pretty Woman, *but I didn't have Richard Gere behind me. I was spending on my Co-op debit card.'*

One Sleeping Bag and No Pans

I know that I've been lucky that sport has allowed me to have a lot of material possessions, but I do remember what it's like to be skint and there have been times in my life when I was just as happy when I had nothing. I wish I could get that across, that you don't need much to be happy.

When I was about 17, I moved into digs in Chorlton, Manchester. I shared with a couple of older lads who were 21–25 at the time. I was so ill-equipped for what was required – I didn't even have a bed, let alone other furniture to make the place feel like home. Crockery, cutlery, bedding, cleaning materials . . . everything was an afterthought. I agreed to take the box room and slept in an old sleeping bag. I'd taken it from my nan's house – it was probably subconsciously giving me some comfort in a wild lifestyle. It's funny how those innocuous items can mean so much; it was all I needed at the time and that period of my life was good fun. Anything more than my cricket kit and a sparse collection of clothes would have been lost on me – they were really happy times because I didn't know any better and felt right at home. I actually found it quite comforting because it reminded me of my own bedroom growing up. It was cosy and I felt safe.

I think it's all too easy for young people to sink into debt with the determination to have the latest gadgets or to overstretch on rent. It might be a few decades since I was that age, but I don't remember a CD Walkman in the same way that sleeping bag has stuck with me. The same could be said of going to our old local, The Quadrant – it wasn't some fancy club bleeding me dry for a round.

Lancashire rented that house for us, which was great but the area was definitely a bit tastier than it is now. Chorlton has been properly gentrified since we lived there. Our place was behind the bus station and I remember going to get some food from the Chinese then sprinting past the gangs who were hanging around, just so I could get home safely.

I was only young but I'd still be going down the Deansgate in the city centre of Manchester with the older lads. We'd go to JW Johnson and prop up the downstairs bar; we'd also go to the first Wetherspoons to open in Manchester, The Moon Under Water.

I never cooked a single meal in the time I lived in Chorlton. Not one. It's not like we were living like animals and it wasn't clean, the lads were actually quite hygienic. They were going out and they were trying to get women to come back, weren't they? So, they had to keep a degree of respectability on the off-chance they had company.

I was still pretty young so that was a bloody eye-opener for me when we were going out all the time and living the life. It was good living together but it also showed me everything I didn't want to be. I remember some of the folk at work telling me not to tell my mum what was going on, and in all honesty, I was pretty shocked by some of it too.

Some nights, I'd go out with the lads from the house and I'd be in places I shouldn't be. It was just as bad when people would end up back at our place at 2am. There would be random folk turning up and if I hadn't been out, I was in my room listening to it and would eventually pop down to see what was going on. The lads would tell me to get back to bed, but that wasn't happening.

It felt like such an important part of growing up – you had to fend for yourself and learn to pick your battles. I look back at it now and there were certain things I wanted to do, and other stuff I knew I didn't like or want to be involved in, and that was so important, working that out for myself.

I think sometimes you think because you're a professional sportsman, the rules don't really apply. It's bizarre. You're put on this pedestal, or you're put in this inflated position that you shouldn't be in. You're only playing a bit of cricket but you can start to think you're a big shot. I was alright because I was always knocking around with older people, but I can completely understand how young professional sportsmen and women can get distracted easily.

When I was playing full-time, when I was about 19, my wage went up to £16,000 a year, so I bought my first house in Preston, and shortly after, Paddy moved in too. It was a tiny three-bedroom, semi-detached new build with paper-thin walls. On one side it was painted a teal green colour, which still sticks with me.

I had the walls painted yellow and a blue carpet fitted before adding bright red leather couches and a big telly. Reading that back, it sounds horrific, but I loved it back then. It was all open-plan because I banged some walls down. The kitchen was obviously brand spanking new, which made it feel a bit special after the Chorlton digs, and I had the other rooms painted lime green when I moved in.

I was wondering what those walls would say if they could talk but actually I'm more worried about what the neighbours could hear! All the walls were so thin. I feel for the people living on that street. When we moved in, I could see it in their eyes – they knew we were going to be a nightmare. We used to come in at all hours. The music would go on and we'd be having barbecues at 4am. We got letters complaining, but at that age we just put it down to them being miserable! It was like, 'What's wrong with people?' Now I realise we were bloody awful.

I remember one rowdy occasion when our mate Andy Bell joined the Marines. The night he left, we went to the nightclub, Legends, which was a tasty club in the car park up at Preston North End. As a send-off, we stripped him naked and tie-wrapped him to the gate of Preston North End. The police came, just gave him a blanket and left! He was there all night, so he wasn't a happy bunny.

That was what it was like all the time, it was bonkers.

We did come off the rails at that point. We'd be out most nights of the week. We found this wine bar in Preston, where we became regulars. There were always drink promotions on and we would take advantage of them – it wasn't a great culture, looking back at all the boozing. On the surface it sounds like a 19-year-old living the dream, and to some extent it was, but on reflection, if I was being honest, I should have been more dedicated to being better on the cricket field. Even though I was performing at an acceptable level, I should have been doing more.

I wouldn't say I outgrew Preston but greener pastures opened up as I started to earn a bit more money. It was at that point I bought a flat on my own in Manchester; it was a loft apartment and I loved it. It gave me some memories off the cricket field, I'll tell you, but it did nothing for my career.

The plan was to live there on my own but my best mate Paddy eventually came with me and it all just started again with the wild nights out in Manchester.

That time of my life, I was bonkers. I don't know if I would trade it looking back. By getting that out of my system it helped me discover who I really was. If I hadn't done it, would I have been a greater cricketer? I think about it more than I should do. When Ronaldo took his shirt off the other night when he played against Ireland, I was never like that. I think if I played now, I would have been practising, training and dedicating myself completely to it. But let's be honest, I wouldn't be who I am had I done that back then. You have options and make mistakes and have decisions with no emotional attachment. It's very easy to say what I would have done. But at that time you make the best decision for you. No point worrying about it now, just make the best decision you can. Maybe that was my way of dealing with it and I did alright.

Getting Paid

I look back to the innocence with which I approached money conversations when I was a teenager. At Lancashire, I had contract meetings and they had a strict pay structure which you didn't go outside. It wasn't competitive with what other people were paying at the time, so when I was offered my contract, I had a big decision to make for a young man. This was different to my first contract, when I was simply so pleased to have received an offer from Lancashire.

That day, Bumble came round my house and made this lovely speech. He said, 'We've come here because we want Andrew to sign. He's everything we want at Lancashire and that's why I've come to see you at home. We're going to pay him £2.5k a year to start with, but that will go up when he makes the second team, and then up again when he becomes a first team player.' We had the good china out. Bourbons, even a few biscuits in foil. We were in the good living room, which never got used unless it was a really special occasion.

It was like I'd won the lottery. It was running through my head – *this is a dream, Bumble's having a brew and a Custard Cream in my house!* As soon as he said he was coming to the house, it was a done deal. He was in our house in Preston. He turned it on for me mum and dad, it was all very nice.

I got to Old Trafford and Bumble took me aside and said, 'All that nice stuff I said to your mum and dad? Do not listen to any of that, I was saying all the right things – I'm going to work you hard now!'

Later on, after I'd established myself, I'd been offered something like £120,000 from a couple of other counties, so there were options for me elsewhere. The chairman said, 'Right, you've played for England. We can put you on the top band of wages.' At the time, I was thinking, *All right, lovely! The county I love putting me straight into the top tier, here we go.*

So, the chairman, smiling away with the club secretary by his side, says, 'Sixty grand.'

I can see myself now, still a teenager, scratching my head and saying, 'Yeah, that's nice, thank you, but I've been offered double that elsewhere.'

He started telling me about the pay structure again, explaining that's how Lancashire did it, going over the same ground. Eventually, I interrupted to go over my ground again, with two counties offering me double that amount.

The chairman just told me to take it then. So, I panicked and said, 'No, no, no! That's not what I'm saying, I don't want to.'

Next thing, I've somehow agreed to the money, contracts are drawn up on official paper and I'm summoned to sign a hard copy. Cricket players didn't have agents back then – in fact, I was one of the first to get one in professional cricket – but at this time, it was just me. Before I signed, I took one last look through the contract for my own peace of mind and I saw that my salary was £55,000. I pointed out what I thought was a typo or a mistake made in the office and the chairman took some pleasure in breaking the news: 'On reflection, son, you didn't quite qualify for the top band so it's £55,000. Take it or leave it.'

MONEY

They knew I wasn't going to leave, so I said, 'Oh, go on then.'

People wonder why sportsmen and women have agents. The next contract I signed, I wasn't even involved in the discussion to avoid that situation happening again. It didn't really matter though because I wasn't paid a penny by Lancashire for eight years – I didn't earn a bean. I signed a contract with them but it would have been as well saying 'Ten pence and a packet of Quavers' on it, or £10m. It didn't really matter then, and it doesn't matter to me now. It is how it is. It was my ECB contract that paid my wages, which meant Lancashire didn't pay me. In any other sport, you'd get something from both, but for some reason it didn't bother me much at the time. For me, it was never about the money: it was about the pride of playing for Lancashire. I didn't move clubs and I still have that pride every time I go to the ground – you can't buy that.

Lancashire had all my image rights and I played for them when I wasn't playing with England. You got nowt, but do you know what? You didn't even question it. I didn't bother because it was happening for me on the pitch, though thinking back to the image rights side of it now, I had been there since I was nine, so if they want to stick my face on a mug and sell it for three quid in the shop, then crack on. They helped me become the player I was and the person I am, so fair enough. Cricket was changing at that time and I was too focused on what was going on off the field rather than what was going on on the grass. My lifestyle wasn't out of control, but it wasn't far off, because I was preoccupied with all the trappings that came with it. I even had to borrow money off my agent Chubby Chandler to pay off my tax bill. I later learned that if I worked hard at my cricket, the rest would take care of itself.

I made my England debut in 1998, the same summer that the English national football team was playing at the World Cup in France. At the same time I was pulling on the jersey in cricket, the world of football was probably reaching a crazy peak of commercial success. David Beckham was exploding on the scene and he had all the adidas deals with image rights across the globe. I remember so much on TV at the time, with the Brazilian team in the airport promoting Nike in the era of Ronaldo, Rivaldo and Ronaldinho.

If you can take anything from my experience, it's talking to people you respect and admire when it comes to big financial decisions. It can be difficult talking money but you have to place trust in someone so you don't drop the ball.

I don't mind sharing the best contract I had with the ECB. They were paying a basic salary of £205,000 a year. By the time you add your match appearances and win bonuses, I was probably earning in the region of £400,000. I have never really concerned myself with what other people earn, especially footballers, because I feel so fortunate for what I earned.

I exceeded, even at that point, anything I ever expected for playing cricket. I was doing the one thing I love and I was getting paid for it. That was perfect to me. Don't get me wrong, I'd have loved to earn footballer's wages, but I didn't begrudge them the money because I was so happy with getting paid for cricket. I still can't believe it.

The money was great to me but every time I went out, I'd try my best. Money wasn't the incentive for me to perform. I wanted to win every game I played, so if the win bonus had been £10 or £10m, I couldn't have tried any harder. I can't recall a game where I was on the field thinking about money as a catalyst to push me on.

After The Ashes of 2005, there was some talk about adopting the Australian model, where they rank players from one to 25, depending on your value to the team. We were sat in the meeting with a presentation and an overhead projector showing our ranking beside our name and what the pay bracket was. I sat there looking around – you could see everyone was trying to work out where they would be. And I knew where I'd be at that point, right at the top.

I was looking at this thing, thinking, *Yeah, I'm in for this. This is amazing.* And everyone else was going, 'Fuck off!' I would have been handed quite a handy pay rise, but some of them would have taken pay cuts so it all got rejected.

Nowadays, the top players are earning about £1m.

I've seen it all in my career – from dodgy builders and financial advisors ripping me off, to borrowing money to pay off tax bills in my early twenties, and what I've learned is these things are complicated. You can't just say, 'take responsibility yourself', you have to put your trust in others. I trusted some of the wrong people, people I thought were friends, who attended my wedding, my children's christenings, but all the time they had their fingers in the till, and they were doing it with a smile on their face. I was burned. I've only just started to trust people in this field again now.

Bidding War

I went through a really unusual experience as a sportsman where I was getting auctioned off in a live bidding war on TV. At the time I happened to be in the West Indies, halfway through a Test match when the auction was going on in India. With the time delay, the event was happening at 3am our time.

You can't go to bed and find out in the morning how things have worked out for you – especially after half the team have gone for a song earlier in the evening. So, I was up all night, watching Rajasthan Royals bidding for me. They were Shane Warne's side and I was thinking it would be a great move for me. The Chennai Super Kings were in for me too and that would have been even better. The fee was going up and up. In the end, I went for $1.55m, which has to go down as a good night's work for sitting on my arse watching a telly in the Caribbean!

I got up the next day after a couple of hours' sleep and found myself feeling incredibly awkward over breakfast. Some of the lads hadn't been bought, a couple of others had gone for peanuts and then there's me and Kevin Pietersen, looking at each other over the cornflakes. We went for the same money at different clubs. I doubt he felt as uncomfortable as I did, though. I couldn't eat my breakfast, it was so painfully awkward. It was living proof at that precise moment in time that money can twist everything.

It would have been nice to go for a quid more than Kevin because we would have been winding each other up about it. In the dressing room, there's a lot of professional jealousy – especially when it came down to money. No beef here. Just fun. Kevin was more of a victim of it when I left. I think Kevin felt it, but we were never in competition like that. Everyone knew what everybody else was getting with England because there was a band system, but then you've got your sponsorship deals built around that, which worked well for me and Kev. When we were all doing well and the team was getting results, people were fine with it. But when we didn't reach expectations, you could hear the rumblings in the dressing room, loud and clear.

I was injured in my first game for the Chennai Super Kings; it felt like something had gone wrong with my knee. If it had been for England, I'd have gone through the pain but I just couldn't do it. I feel horrible admitting it, but I only played three games and never went back.

The Value of Money

The other week, I was looking at houses and an estate agent was showing me round some property in Cheshire. I asked how much this one house was going for and he showed me the price.

A footballer was going round the house after me, followed by a couple of other household names in football. The estate agent actually said, 'The list price is significantly higher for them, Fred.'

I wanted to leave straight away. How can you justify that? Just preying on them because they've got a few quid. But that's the way the world is now. It made me wonder if there was a premium added because I'm on the telly.

Everyone sees you in a certain light, particularly when it comes to money – they just assume you've got bundles of it at all times. I have spunked a fair amount in my time as well as put my trust in people I maybe shouldn't have, including financial advisors, but you realise at a certain point in life you have to take care of your own situation and really have ownership of it.

We bought a piece of land and built a house. I was paying the builder who wasn't paying the workmen and it was funding his other projects. They then went bust on me. I didn't know if I had to pay the lads, but I wanted to, so I paid twice to cover the tradesman. It was such a state that I had to pay double than what was agreed. This builder was up and running and soon after I bumped into him in a coffee shop. He seemed to have no remorse at all. You can't win, you are automatically wrong if you do something dramatic. If I had done anything, it would have gone wrong for me. He hasn't just slapped my arse, he's tanned it. There was nothing I could do. It bothered me for so long and it still does. It was over ten years ago. The money I had earned, playing through injuries, and a man had just robbed it off me. I can't square that away easily and there is nothing I can do. I just hope there is such a thing as karma.

Money changes people so much. I've seen it so many times. People I've worked with in business who have ripped me off purely through greed. It's so sad when people measure success almost solely based on what's in their bank account.

Over the past year, I've started making investments again through other people for the first time in a long while. I'm working with my best mate, Paddy. Not just because he's my best mate, you understand, but because he's a financial advisor. Everyone will tell you that mixing business and friendship can affect relationships badly, but I've done so with people I don't know and then become friends with them while they were ripping me off. I'd sooner have someone I trust implicitly, who treats it as his own money with an emotional attachment to my kids and everyone around me. If we're in it together, we're in it together as mates. We don't mention anything outside of a working environment but when we have a meeting, we get dressed appropriately, bring our computers and have proper meetings. It's working well for us.

However, money is not the be-all and end-all. I think people measure it wrongly and I know that I've been guilty of this in the past. When you're so focused on chasing money, you convince yourself it's because you want to provide security. I find it hard to turn a job down when there's a great fee attached but at the same time, that formula means you're missing out on really important stuff: a premium comes with that, it's a sacrifice.

All the way through my career, I've missed out on a lot of stuff with the kids – the boys playing cricket or spending quality time with my daughter. During my cricket career, I was often there, but I wasn't always present. And yet true success to me is when you sit around your dinner table at home and everyone is smiling. If they are all happy and talking to each other, those are the moments I feel like we've done well.

I think I've got that now, to a point. Everyone strives to do well when they have kids and hopes for the best, but nobody is perfect. We all make big mistakes, but that's also a huge part of developing and learning.

MONEY

I want my kids to do something that excites them, something they're passionate about and really into. Hopefully, I'm in a position as a parent where I can help with that.

I'm weird with money. Some stuff, I get really tight about. I don't know if it's a working-class thing, but I know what I want to pay for something and I can feel the natural reflex taking over if someone is at it. It's things that don't cost much sometimes. It took me three years to get Amazon Prime. I love boxing but pay per view fights? No. Why have I got to pay more? I don't want to pay more for boxing. I am at odds with myself at the minute. I loved Matchroom Boxing on Sky. I can't bring myself to pay £2 for DAZN. I really like Eddie, he's funny, but why £2 a month? No. I'm going to have it out with him when I see him. I have been a loyal supporter on Sky and he wants two more of my well-earned pounds? He puts fights on in his garden just to show you where your £2 is going. He's got a massive house! No wonder you're always smiling and speaking out the side of your mouth, Ed!

If I've got an idea of what something should cost, I can't go over it. I know things are worth more or less to different people. If I go over what I think something is worth, I'm always going to have that in my head – that I paid more than I wanted to – and I wouldn't be able to enjoy it. I've missed out on cars by a few hundred quid because there's a point I just won't go above. Not even a pound. I've also done it with T-shirts, shoes, trainers and holidays.

I haggle for everything. When we used to tour Pakistan, I'd spend nights in the hotel shops, looking at rugs and haggling with the guys because I could pass three hours like that. You'd get a few cups of tea and have a laugh in the process – you end up buying a rug, just to thank them for passing the time. And it helped me get through those tours – haggling over three quid for an hour.

Spending It

As kids, we would get shoes from a place called Tommy Ball's. There was one in Blackburn and one in Preston. I remember this pair of trainers I wanted – black Nike Air Max. They were my size and they had a pink swoosh on them – I fell in love with the idea of wearing them. I couldn't afford them at the time, they were £120 even back then. That was a good £100 over what I was paying for a pair of trainers.

That exact pair that I'd fallen in love with were in the storeroom of Champion Sports in Debenhams, where I did my work experience. I contemplated nicking them every day but I never did. I would have been a bad thief because it would have played on my mind too much and I'd have been seen knocking about in them. I never got them, so I turned my attention to Travel Fox, which were pretty garish-looking.

We would also go shopping at the first B&M Bargains, which opened in Fleetwood. One over from Blackpool, Fleetwood is like a fishing town, not a very affluent place. My Auntie Joan used to take us with my mum in the back of her Mk2 Ford Escort. We would walk through the town centre and there was a sports shop on the way there. This pair of Travel Fox trainers were in the window and I used to walk past wishing I could afford them. They were £80, properly aspirational for a Preston lad and the best things I'd ever seen, brilliant white. Then one day, Sports Direct got them in for £30 – but they didn't have my size. I nearly bought a different size just to have a pair.

It might sound mad, but that experience of not being able to afford something I wanted so badly was something I never shook off. So now, Nike Air Jordans have become an addiction, some might say (Rachael, if you're reading) – even though they're £110 a pair, they are worth more than gold to me. When I was growing up, I couldn't have them; I simply couldn't afford them. Now I've got all these pairs, still in boxes unworn, because it's an echo of my childhood. I just put them on in the house because if I get them dirty, it will ruin my day. I'll sometimes buy two pairs of the same shoe, one for wearing and one for keeping. When I start buying a third pair, that's a sign it will be a real problem.

I'm looking at cars and it sounds terrible but if I wanted to,

I could afford some pretty special vehicles – within reason. But what I want is very different. I've got a Ferrari at the minute, a 458, and I love it. It's nine years old and it's lost more than half of its value. I could never have bought a brand new edition of a Ferrari – a car costing more than my mum and dad's house?!

I feel conflicted about it. When I drive it, I'm acutely aware of what I'm driving. I love cars and I've loved the brand since I was a kid. It doesn't stop you feeling embarrassed when you pull up in certain places. I would rarely take it to Preston. You pull up at petrol stations and people comment and I find myself playing it down or making excuses for the car. It probably suggests I shouldn't have it, but on the flip side I love it. I used to have a Lamborghini but I kept it in the garage. I was too big for it, it kept getting bumped on my drive because it was too low. I'd go in the garage and look at it like it was a piece of art. I couldn't bring myself to drive it because I'd feel such a knobhead in it.

So, if I ever wanted one, I would wait ten years until it's a sensible price. Even this 458, I drive it round and as much as I love Ferrari, and I genuinely do, part of me doesn't enjoy it. I just don't feel that I should be in it, I feel that it's making a statement and it's one I don't want to make – I feel genuinely awful in it. So I've sold it. I've got a Land Rover Defender on the drive now, it chugs about and I love it.

MONEY

This might be getting a bit *Top Gear*, this chat, but I'm looking at a 1996 BMW M3 Evolution. They're 15 grand, which is probably more realistic in my head from when I was growing up. I'm looking at cars like that with more excitement than if I could buy a Bugatti because when I was a kid, starting to drive and wanting to pass my test, the BMW was the car I looked at and thought, *That's what I want, that's what I really want.* It's the same with a 355 Ferrari, which you can pick up for decent money now.

The missus tears her hair out with it. She doesn't understand. She says, 'If you want a car, why don't you buy the best car and just get one?'

The best car in the wider world isn't the best car to me. I nearly bought a big BMW 750 as my runaround for 12 grand. I'm not even a Bond fan, but it was the 750iL, which was in James Bond. That's stuck with me from my youth and that's why I wanted it.

It's so weird. Clothes are the same for me. I can't go over a certain price with T-shirts but then I take my mates out or I go out for food and I don't care at all. If I get an experience like when I go away with my mates that's worth a lot to me, I'll book an Airbnb for all of us and I don't even think about it. So why do I then try to save a fiver somewhere else?

I remember I bought a suit from Armani when I shouldn't have done. I got well and truly sucked in when I was 17. It cost

£400 and I can't forgive myself for it. It didn't even fit, it was really baggy on the shoulders. There were some lovely girls in there working as sales assistants, I was young and naïve when I went in, the lads make you feel like you shouldn't be in there. It was all a bit *Pretty Woman*. But I didn't have Richard Gere behind me, I was spending on my Co-op debit card. It didn't stop me going back and buying the same jacket in two different colours. I've still got buyer's remorse 27 years on. I looked like Rodney Trotter in them.

I've got some jewellery – there's the earrings, which I'll melt down for Rachael or my daughter. I've got some watches but nothing like some of the dads at the school gates.

I've got some watches and they were all gifts from Rachael, which mean something special to me because she knows I couldn't bring myself to spend a serious amount of money on a watch. I don't really wear them now, I feel too flash. I've got one that's way over the top from Cartier. This fella used to come round and sell watches – I'm pretty sure it's real! He used to do it in his car and he would go round all the footballers. He used to visit Paul Dickov, the former Scotland and Man City striker, across the road from us. Paul put him on to me and I ended up with this Cartier Diamond watch. I got a good deal on it, it wasn't stupid money. I wore it to Elton John's White Tie and Tiara Ball. When I was sat with Elton, I went to check the time. He looked at the watch and said, 'That's a nice watch but it's very camp.' I had my hands in my pockets for the rest of the night, big diamond earring in as well.

I've gone the other way with everything. Often I've found that when I've bought myself something in the past, it was to hide something else that was going on. I suffer terribly from buyer's remorse. In 2008, I was going to buy a Bentley so I went in the showroom and set the whole deal up and ordered the car. I said to myself, 'If I get a hundred for England, I'll buy it.' But I never got the century so I didn't get the car. I stuck to it and was pleased I did.

I think it's good to have an idea of what you're happy to pay for stuff and be disciplined in sticking to that, but I do think it's really important to buy things when you've earned the money and you deserve a reward. So, don't be like me in that respect: it's special to feel good about that and enjoy it.

CHAPTER EIGHT

MENTAL HEALTH

*'If someone asks you how you are feeling,
don't be afraid to tell them the truth.'*

Fitting In

I don't like being told what I should like. I spent too long doing that – too long conforming and playing the game. As you get older, it's more comfortable to use your age as an excuse to say 'no' more often or be blunt about disliking something.

Something that really damages my impression of something is hype. If someone's banging on about something being so brilliant, I know it's not going to live up to my expectations. I know I'm going to be disappointed. You definitely come to understand these things in your forties. I've got to go into something with a modest view, thinking it might be all right. Then if it's good, it's a huge bonus and if not, it's what I thought.

I thought the Ricky Gervais series *After Life* (2019–) was going to fall into the category of over-hype and yet another brisk dismissal from me. Even then, I had to wait a year to watch it so all the hype had calmed down.

I've never met Ricky Gervais but the sentiment of the

series really hit me. The pitching of the dark humour alongside the brutality of grief and the struggle that comes from losing someone was perfect. Ricky has a brilliant brain and his humour really appeals to me. I liked his series *Derek* (2012–14) as well, which some people took a furious dislike to – I think that made me like it even more. The way criticism bounces off him is so inspirational; we could all learn a thing or two from him about a thick skin.

I find it hard when friends or people you know or you follow on social media are constantly hammering people you know and like. It puts you in a bit of an awkward predicament. I've seen it a few times, where I'm weighing up the impact of having a word about it.

If you are ever seeking a retweet from someone famous, drop Ricky a compliment on *Derek*. He must love that programme because he's always discussing it. The series is all about mental health and people can be offended easily when it's challenged in comedy. But as someone who suffers from issues myself, I think it's quite refreshing; it shows a nice side to it and an innocence that most people shy away from.

Derek's vulnerability in that series talks to me because I'm actually painfully awkward at times. People who recognise me from cricket assume I'm a domineering personality. That idea of being an alpha male is a concept in life we should question and challenge. Don't get me wrong, there were times in my career when it wasn't an act – and I loved it. I would be running in and I'm bowling in front of 25,000 people. Unashamedly, I loved it. I genuinely thrived on the gladiatorial nature of it. In that moment you forget about everything else in the world because nothing else matters. You feel like you can do anything, it's brilliant. But there are times when it's false bravado, a mask for other problems that you're putting off dealing with. I was always told when walking out to bat, don't put on your helmet until you are in the middle. It's a display of confidence, a puffing of the chest and a way to show you're not scared or intimidated. So, I always did that.

The truth for me is that I was always hiding. I may not have been as technically gifted as some of the other players but I was dogged and I found ways to win. I could intimidate people, use my size and presence even though I don't see myself as the least bit intimidating. I could give off that aura of confidence and power.

The family have noticed it in me. They will see me on TV, in front of an audience or dicking about with Jamie Redknapp on *A League of Their Own*. To the wider world I'm always having a laugh or doing something upbeat that requires me to be the life and soul of the party but the family see me at home, where they see every side of me, and the two don't marry up. They see you when you are happy, sad, angry or depressed and they've seen the difference in me without a doubt. I am quite open with them about it, but it's still an area where I need to improve. It's one of the key lessons I've learned and would advise anyone to embrace. Talk to people about how you are feeling, it's amazing how it helps. Let them know if you're having a rough ride and if you're feeling down. It is good to talk – there's a reason that has become a strapline for mental health, because when you get things out there and talk about them, it really helps. It's not a cliche. It truly works.

Embarrassment is a thing that holds people back so much but once you start embracing being embarrassed about something, it settles down and doesn't last long. It's tied into this idea of putting yourself out of your comfort zone and pushing through feeling uncomfortable – like the Andros Townsend effect I was talking about earlier (*see also* p.94). Whatever it is, whether it's something silly or profound, once you've done it, it's like all these things, you suddenly have another layer of experience. I think it's all linked to our mental health – once you've pushed yourself through it, there's a freedom that follows. There must be a release of serotonin or adrenalin in the brain that helps quell depression.

I'm not suggesting everyone goes out and starts amateur dramatics, it could be the smallest thing. Check yourself the next time you feel that anticipation or anxiety and remind yourself of the reward waiting on the other side. I can only describe it as liberating. I think I've found some sort of freedom – to a point.

Depression

I started a public conversation about my own experience with mental health when I made the BBC documentary *Hidden Side of Sport* in 2012. And I'm pleased I did, but I look back on it now and have some reservations about how we handled one sportsman in particular who agreed to talk to us about their own troubles.

I still think about the way we interviewed Graeme Dott, the former snooker world champion. We arrived at his house in Scotland and we had such a good laugh with him and so much fun. His missus came in with a drinks tray and, I kid you not, she had cans of Irn-Bru stacked up and loads of Tunnock's stuff – straight from central casting of a happy Scottish family who made a living in a sport like snooker – all that was missing was a Krankie.

Graeme was loving life and he was happily filming with us on his practice table. Our director, and my good pal Gabe Turner from the production company Fulwell 73, had the job of trying to bring the conversation round to why we were there: to discuss Graeme's struggles with depression in sport.

You could see as he started to tell his story his shoulders were dropping and his head was going down. Just discussing how hard it had been to cope with the limelight and glare of attention was sucking the life out of him. We dragged him down in order to tell the story we needed for the documentary.

After filming, we were booked in to go to Satty Singh's, a famous Glasgow curry house. We didn't ask Graeme along. I can picture it now – we're backing up, reversing out of his drive, and he's standing at his snooker table in a converted garage, waving us off. To this day, I wonder why we didn't ask him to come with us for a curry – it's not like we didn't want him there, it was just an oversight. It bothers me.

With Graeme, as a snooker player, he had that pressure of playing in front of the camera with no team-mates for support, for hours on end. It's either the best place in the world when things are going your way or the loneliest, most exposed you could ever be. We should have taken him out and thanked him properly, perhaps that would have helped? I regret things like that in life and I'd like to put it right – I'd love to take him to Satty Singh's now – so Graeme, I'll fix that.

The first time I witnessed depression first-hand, I didn't really understand what was going on. I didn't have the understanding or vocabulary to express it, although it was obvious something wasn't right.

It was the early 2000s and we were on tour. Steve Harmison was struggling, really struggling. You knew he was having

MENTAL HEALTH

real problems because his mood would dip so much, you couldn't help noticing it. It wasn't like anything I'd seen; it wasn't a sadness, it was this vacant atmosphere around him. There was an emptiness, like he wasn't completely present. It was a clinical depression – and very few of us knew what was going on.

I didn't know about mental health or depression when I was a teenager, it wasn't part of the conversation in competition during my development. It was all so frighteningly simple to me back then. If I was on it with my cricket, I'll get you out or score runs. If you're on it, you'll get me out or score runs.

To give you an idea of how daft we were back then, I used to nick Steve's pills – I would call them 'eggs' – and neck them. They helped me sleep. They didn't half make me feel a bit better! It was no wonder, they were proper prescription pills. In the end, I'd just say, 'Go on, Steve. Give us one of your eggs.' He'd just say, 'Yeah, go on then.' Whether it was a placebo thing or they actually worked, I don't know, but I had a fair few on tour of Pakistan and India.

If I'm truly honest, I didn't understand what he was going through but I could identify with the symptoms he was showing. I have this recollection of him being on the floor or in his bed, sleeping or dozing. He wouldn't get up for hours, this lethargy following him about. Even in the dressing room, he would be sat down all the time or even lying down.

People thought that was lazy but I was thinking, *There's something up here.*

I knew, because I had it too.

Harmy found it hard to leave home, which we all put down to homesickness on the tours and trips we'd been on. Initially, we would all get it. But there was something else too: you could sense it was eroding him as a person and suffocating his confidence. You could see it in the way he carried himself. It was visible in the way he would talk as well – he just wasn't with it during a conversation. He had a look on his face that was telling you something wasn't right and it had to be addressed.

It's a vicious circle. The 'lazier' you are – in other words, the more lethargic you feel – the worse your eating habits become. Me and Harmy would eat chocolate, just sat watching telly all day. Seeing hours of the day go by and not really getting involved in what other people were doing. Fortunately for us both, we've come through those times, but we're still a work in progress. Though it took me ages to truly understand what Harmy went through; mental health just wasn't being discussed 20 years ago, so it was all new to us then.

Other players have been brave enough to talk about it but it's their story and not for me to take into this conversation. Depression in cricket was suddenly taken seriously after players started going home from tour because they couldn't

MENTAL HEALTH

face being away any longer. The life we were leading was damaging to our mental health, there's no denying it now. It was completely routine and expected that you would miss the birth of your children if the dates clashed with a tour. I can only compare it to being in the Armed Forces – life had to go on back home if you had an important mission abroad. You could be away for three months at a time. But then also, the reaction towards it made me think, *I can never tell anyone about how I feel.*

The press wrote about Harmy as if he was lazy, as if he was struggling with homesickness and had to get a grip. It was painted like he was a bad egg. Which is mad because out of everyone I played with, bar none, Steve is the best. He is selfless – he would get himself in shit or find himself with all sorts of problems to help someone else. And he should have spent more time on himself because it never came back to him from a lot of people. But the press hammered him. And they came up with all these reasons why he was the way he was without attempting to find out what was going on or explain how difficult things had become for him. It's just a relief he came through it.

With my own depression, of course I don't control it. That's not how it works. But I find ways of getting through it. I've seen psychologists and a series of therapists over the years and they have helped. There are certain triggers. If I get lazy, if I don't keep active, don't keep a routine, that's when I know I'm susceptible to a bout of depression. There are ways to control or prevent it. There are things I can do to minimise the risk. Having said that, things can be going perfectly, and then it could just hit me. It's not straight forward. I was on medication for years but came off it. It is a bit of a taboo for people. Why is mental health any different from taking paracetamol for a headache? If you feel mentally ill or are struggling, go and see a therapist. For me, you have to normalise it. People don't question going to see a physio for an injury, it has to be the same for your head. It goes against the grain a little but I will actually have a chat with myself. I will tell myself to get it together and that method, that process, works for me. Sometimes I've had to become someone else to tackle certain situations. Looking back, that's what I did with cricket. But equally, trying to be a good version of myself for other people has also helped. Give your kids and partner, or friends and family, someone to believe in. Don't be flaky, be dependable. I've said it so many times in this book: you have to be yourself.

    I've found that, for me, working helps. Whenever the black cloud is hanging over me, I've always managed to pick myself up and get into work. I know I've got to do something if I'm going to feel better. Whatever I'm feeling inside, if I can get to work then usually, by the end of the day, I do start to feel a little bit better. I think mainly because it forces me to get out, be around other people and not isolate, which for me, is dangerous. Routine is massive. I'd say that if you're struggling, if you possibly can, just getting up in the morning and doing something as menial as brushing your teeth, having a wash and getting out of the house for a walk can make everything seem better. Or at least it's a start. Though please don't think I'm preaching or telling you what to do, this is what has worked for me.

Giving Up the Booze

I used to love drinking but not all the time: I stopped because it was becoming a problem, simple as that. It was the right thing to do. A friend of mine said recently, 'There are some people who give up drinking who should never have given up. There are others who definitely should have.' I put myself in the latter. It was the right time for me. I don't know if I'll ever drink again, but right now, I don't want to. The lesson is about living in the present. The thought of being a 75-year-old man sat at a bar with a dog at my feet drinking a Heineken zero isn't how I planned it, but I know I do want to get to 75 and if I carry on drinking that dog might be sat on his own. That's my thing and I'm not going to make anyone else feel uncomfortable about it.

I'm not one of the preachers: people who have stopped

drinking and want to tell you why you should. So, if I do tell you, it's definitely not small talk! And I'm not one of those people when you buy a round, who can't just ask for a Diet Coke, they feel the need to tell you they don't drink. I wasn't asking that: just have your Diet Coke, it's all good. It's the same with vegetarian food. Just order your food, don't tell me your requirements. I'll go into my pocket, look and say to them, sorry I've run out of medals. I'm not bothered about why you've chosen that life.

I've tried it all. I've been to meetings, which initially worked for me because you realise it's not just you. I stopped going to them because I didn't feel the need to drink or want to drink. In some ways those meetings were a reminder. If it's sport, life or work – I don't believe that one size fits all which is a departure from what I used to think. You have to find what works for you. There's nothing wrong with trying a few outfits on. The number of people who say they can't work me out. Take people for what they are. You don't have to understand everything, just respect people for being different. I guess I've taken pointers from all different places and put them together in a way that has worked for me.

I'm sure a lot of people who give up drinking come from the default position that things were always bad. I don't really fit that mould because for me, a lot of it was absolutely brilliant. When I think of all of the incredible nights I've had, I

MENTAL HEALTH

don't regret many of them. The bad times were bad, don't get me wrong, and they make me cringe looking back now. It's nothing to be proud of. You have to address them, acknowledge the mistakes and see why it all went tits up.

I went out with people I used to drink with and I was bored, to be brutally honest. They don't have to change, it's their choice entirely but I became aware I was sitting watching people get absolutely hammered and I was just as annoying as they were.

When I was drinking, the problem for me lay in the cover-up. I was boozing to try to change the way I felt and that's when it became a problem. If I latched on, I would get into drinking – and not just for one session. It would go on for weeks and that couldn't continue. I never got on with the idea of drinking in the morning, or drinking on my own, which would have made my problems even bigger. The volume I could pack away was a big worry, it was time to stop.

Trust has been a big struggle for me and has become a bigger issue the older I get. Stopping drinking was a big moment because boozing was hindering my ability to trust the right people. Decision making was part of it, but I was becoming a person I didn't want to be. Drinking was holding me back in a sense. Since I've stopped drinking, I am far better at a lot of things. Drinking wasn't making me happy. I was drinking to try and make myself feel better – self-medicating in a way –

but it was having the opposite effect. Stopping has made me happier. And it's made me look better too – which is something I never thought I'd hear myself say out loud.

Bulimia

There was so little support available when I was still playing professional sport. Early on in my career, I plucked up the courage to speak to a senior player to say I was making myself sick after meals. He just replied, 'You'll be alright, lad.' But I didn't give up there, I also attempted to speak to a dietitian about it and she pissed on my chips as well (no pun intended) – I was brushed off completely. I told the medical professionals in the field of nutrition and mental health about that when I was making my 2020 documentary about bulimia, *Living with Bulimia*, and they were pretty shocked. But at the same time, I wouldn't say they were surprised.

I've been as good as gold recently with my eating. I'm by no means conventional or traditional when it comes to eating, but I'm comfortable with it. The problem for me was during the last lockdown when I was doing the documentary, I was actually shocked by how much weight I had lost when I watched it back. I looked really skinny. I wasn't 'at it' being sick – the truth of the matter is, I felt like I was becoming addicted to Peloton, which in itself is a form of bulimia. I thought bulimia was being sick, but it could also be the act of draining myself on the bike. I was training really hard on my own and at the time I was really happy with how I felt. But I look back on it now and think, *Hang on a minute*. It was extreme. I've put a bit of weight back on since then, I feel like I can't win with a steady position on it.

I had abs in the past and I'd find myself looking in the mirror, wondering what happens now? Where do you take it from here? It takes serious commitment to keep that level of body fat down so the muscle shows. I got under 100kg and that was a big deal for me. I was 98kg or 99kg and it was a bit of a let-down. I don't know what it was, but I expected something that never came. I went to the mirror and looked at my abs. It was like finding a unicorn, I'd found the pot of gold at the end of the rainbow. Tensed them, pushed them out, proper six pack. Then felt nothing. This was when I was boxing, three months of a diet, I had trained harder than I had in my life, I got punched in the head for 45 minutes five times a week and suddenly I'm not even that bothered about having abs. Don't get me wrong. I'd love them back but now I know it is an anti-climax.

I love my food, so something had to give. And it was the abs.

My best friends reacted to the documentary I made about eating disorders in exactly the way I hoped and expected they would by ripping the piss out of me. It happened just as I imagined it – 'So are you chucking up after we eat then, mate?' There's one lad, and we had played golf together. I had a sausage roll, flapjack and a cup of coffee. He joked to the lads to keep an eye on me because I might chuck up behind a tree. Some people might find that offensive but I didn't. I just saw it as my mates knowing what I was going through and that's the way they dealt with it, by making fun of it, by saying to me in their own unique way, 'Fred, don't worry, it's fine – we're here.' Don't get me wrong, if a stranger had said it I'd reckon he'd have got a drive around the head, but from a mate it was perfect.

Grief

My grandpa died while I was writing this book. He went downhill really quickly and we were there with him at the end. His name was Henry Hargreaves – although everyone called him Harry – he was 93 years young and he was my mum's dad. We were so close to my nan and grandpa, we would see them all the time when I was growing up. They were there for me ever since I can remember and such a big support during my playing career.

My dad played on a Saturday and every single week they would be there, helping with the teas, chipping in where they were needed. Grandpa helped around the ground and would be sat with us kids all the time, talking about the game. Now and then I stayed at their place in my sleeping bag – the one

MENTAL HEALTH

which came with me into my digs, years later. They were there so consistently in the early days of my career. Nan suffered terribly with claustrophobia and she was frightened of so many things that she couldn't travel. When I started to play international cricket, they watched everything on TV but the notion of getting on a plane or anything like that was just too much for them.

Harry was such an honest fella. He was a builder and site manager by trade and when I look back on the stability he gave me, it was a huge part of my life and the foundation for everything I achieved as an adult. I'm indebted to them really, so if you still have your grandparents, make sure you let them know how much they matter. The older generation just want a bit of company and appreciation, it's not a lot to give them that.

I remember speaking to my grandparents about how they brought us all up – all the funny stories. I get this now, being a parent myself. It's special recounting all those memories and it's good for them to do so. Grandpa used to reminisce about the old days when I was 10, when I was 13, when I was 15 – all of those stories about watching us play cricket. I'm not sure he enjoyed the professional stuff as much.

Even at the end, the second-to-last time I saw him, he was sat in his chair and he was going in and out a little bit. I walked in and he said, 'Have you got a game tomorrow?'

I told him, 'No, not tomorrow, Grandpa. I got a day off tomorrow.'

He smiled, 'Ah, good, good, good.'

Did he still think I was playing cricket?

Way back when I was a kid, Manchester United, Everton and England star Phil Neville was in the year above me at Lancashire and a better cricketer, no doubt about that. He was offered the same contract as me but he signed for Manchester United instead so I took the money – £2,500 a year – the year after. I asked Grandpa if he remembered Phil and his face lit up, 'Oh, Philip. Oh, what a player! What a batter, left-handed. Bet you were glad he stopped!'

I couldn't believe it – he remembered that from 30-odd years ago.

But the painful thing was that two minutes later, he just didn't make any sense about something that was happening right now. It's almost like you grieve twice: when their personality slips away and then when they actually pass.

Grandpa was in a home at this point. Prior to that he'd been in hospital following a fall that had broken his hip. The hospital was challenging because no one could visit due to Covid. That's the other thing about when people get older: what's the right thing to do with them? It was really difficult having conversations about the logistics of a loved one while they're sitting in an ambulance not far from you and you're

MENTAL HEALTH

making decisions about where they should be. Eventually, you become a parent to your parents.

That's a strange one.

Grandpa went into a home so we could guarantee he received the best care possible. His mate was in the same place, so it wasn't full of strangers. He used to visit his pal before he went in, so he knew all the staff and they looked after him when he was there. So, when it reached the point for him, in he went happily.

I went to see him one week and he was alright. Five days later, I got a phone call to go back and he was like a skeleton in bed. He died later that night.

This sounds really weird, because I'm comfortable around death. I can process the physical departure of someone in my head because it's completely natural. That said, I can completely understand and sympathise with people who find grief so difficult to process.

When I was young, there was a lad at the cricket club, Nigel Beatty, who died and I was only about ten (Nigel would have been about 18). There was a nightclub in the Preston Docks called The Manxman and he fell off a wall and drowned. That was the first time I recall a funeral for someone so young.

The cricketer Ben Hollioake was a mate of mine. He died in Australia in a car crash when he was only 24. We toured together in India, got home and said our goodbyes. I remember him leaving and that was the last time I saw him. Just as I was walking out to bat against New Zealand in Wellington in 2002 I found out he had died. That hit us really hard because Ben was something special. He was cool, he was good-looking – he had absolutely everything. I drank really heavily after that, I think we all did. It was my first experience of feeling that gut-wrenching grief, it still gets me now.

The strange thing with me is that when big things happen, I'm pretty good at keeping it together. But it's the little things that can send me out of kilter. With Ben, we drank and we celebrated his life and we reached a point where we came to terms with his death. I still see Adam, his brother, and I actually find that much harder because it stirs up all the emotions you thought you had dealt with.

It was such a different experience when an older relative like my Auntie Ennis died. Of course it was upsetting, but she was older so it felt less shocking. And, in the end, when people are ill, you just want them to go peacefully. But when each of my grandparents died, I felt a mixed emotion of grief and relief. You didn't want them to be suffering or in pain.

When people die, there's a rush for those who are left behind to post 'rest in peace' on social media, often for someone they've never met in their life. But that's the thing, I don't want to feel obliged to do that because it isn't authentic to me. It doesn't feel meaningful sticking up some words with a picture – I'd rather pay my respects in person or privately.

When my Uncle Ted died, it was a relief my Auntie Ennis had gone before him. She would have been livid about what unfolded . . .

We got to the funeral and the extended family were there in force. The hearse pulled up outside the church and I was one of the pallbearers, so we carried him to the head of the congregation, then carried him out afterwards down to the plot in the graveyard next to Ennis. We got there, with him on our shoulders in the coffin, but there was no hole!

So, I was looking at it and I said to my brother, Chris, 'Where are we putting him? There's no hole.' Everyone followed us and the vicar was standing there. I said the same thing to him – 'Mate, where are we putting him? There's no hole?'

He started flapping and this fella came over apologising, 'Oh, so sorry! We forgot to dig the hole.'

So, we had to take him back into the church. Everyone went in and we were all just stood there, so I said, 'Why don't we go and have the wake, go to the pub and come back? It's only down the road.' So off we went and everyone got tanked up. We were all saying, 'Do you think he'll be all right in there on his own in church?'

I said, 'He's not going anywhere, is he? We're going to put him in the ground soon.'

We had to go back to church, all pissed up. And then we had to carry him, by which point they'd got a digger and dug a hole. Fucking hell, one job! Still, he would have had a laugh about it and often that's the best way to find acceptance with grief – find something to make you happy about that person and cherish it.

Grieve for the person and not the time because the memories last forever.

EPILOGUE

HOME

'Nobody else can make the move for you.'

In just two decades life has changed so much for me from when I first moved out of home and had my mate Pete and the community at Lancashire looking out for me in the madness of Chorlton and the loft apartment in Manchester's Deansgate, to meeting Rachael and making our life together. But I still feel like a working-class lad. Often I find myself in mad situations where I have to pinch myself.

I was in New York with Jack Whitehall, James Corden and Jamie Redknapp a couple of years ago and we went out for dinner with one of Jamie's friends, who is a billionaire. After dinner, we went for drinks in a club. Now, this club wasn't my natural habitat. It was the kind of place where the music blares out and drinks at a table set you back a couple of grand. It was hot, I was sweating. There was a queue for one unisex toilet that was about 30 people deep. At the table, they were chucking it down: champagne, Don Julio tequila, Grey Goose vodka, the whole works. I wouldn't have minded, but they're amateurs at this game. The professional has retired – I was supping on a can of Red Bull. Jamie said we should split the bill between the three of us to say thanks to his pal for taking us out. He hadn't taken us out. If he'd taken us out, he'd be paying, but we were paying. That's us taking him out. I was pressured into taking my First Direct card out of my wallet and placing it on a tray next to three Coutts cards, which, if you don't know, is the same bank the Queen uses. As I was processing buying the world's most expensive can of Red Bull, to my delight, the waitress returned with my First Direct Card and asked, 'Which is Mr Flintoff?' My card had been declined and it actually made me feel quite pleased because the other two could easily afford it and something told me the amount we were paying didn't feel like something a lad from Preston should be spending! Don't get me wrong, I completely owned it and laughed about it. The old First Direct bank card was burning up! I don't think Tracey in the call centre was used to calling up and asking for permission for a bill from the *Harper's Bazaar* Fashion Week party to go through from the scene in New York.

It's a mad, conflicting feeling because I also love the food and seeing those places. The Arts Club in Mayfair, London is everything that would normally make my blood boil and my teeth itch. It's full of incredibly wealthy folk but it drives me insane how much I love it. It's quite intimidating to go in. Imagine me going in there when I was younger, in the Preston days or even the Chorlton digs? They just wouldn't have been down with that guy at all. Now, they'll open the door for me and roll out the red carpet even though I'm not even a member. It's preposterous and that's why I love it.

I know the man on the door and we have a chat but all I can hear is an inner monologue telling me, *This is everything I'm not*. But I still like it. The food is magnificent. I love steak tartare – raw steak with an egg in it. You might remember an episode of *Mr Bean* back in the nineties where he's in a restaurant, trying to hide the meat because he has no idea it's raw and can't cope with the shame of admitting he ordered the wrong thing. I love raw meat so I'll have that or I'll go to the Japanese restaurant upstairs instead.

I'm sat looking around and I know at heart, I'm nothing like these people. I don't want to be like them either. But the food is something else. I have somehow infiltrated this new world and it makes me laugh. I'm not sure if they want me around but in a weird way, I like being there. It's bonkers. Noel Gallagher once said in an interview that he's always waiting for someone to come up to him with a clipboard and say, 'Right, Mr Gallagher, you've had enough fun now. Time to go back to Burnage and the dole.'

I get the same feeling when I've been't Hollywood. I've been over there working a lot now but I'm always expecting that tap on the shoulder to remind me what time the last train to Preston is.

The first time I went for work was in 2011 when I was filming the documentary on depression and I interviewed the actor Vinnie Jones. He was so welcoming, it felt like a sunny day at his house in Watford. Then you realise the film director Quentin Tarantino is living next door and you're on Mulholland Drive and it's a different world.

The next time I was over for work was in 2016 with *A League of Their Own* when James Corden sorted the trip. James was still trying to make his way and no one knew who he was out there really, apart from the odd person. We went to a few places like Soho House in West Hollywood and it was nice.

The second time around was totally different. His world had changed massively and now it was a case of access all areas for all of us – we could get where we wanted to go because James' career had gone stratospheric. We went out with David Beckham, we went to his house and then on to the football. It was bizarre. We went to see LA Galaxy. He didn't think he'd be playing so he'd been surfing all morning and he was called up!

You could have rubbed his foot marks out of the centre circle. They just kept passing it to him and he kept spraying balls all over the field. He was taking control and hardly broke a sweat because he was so good. James and I were in his box with Jamie Redknapp and Jack Whitehall. It wasn't all glamorous, John Bishop was out there on holiday with Jason Manford,

HOME

(yes, you have just read that right) which seems like the most unusual group to be in LA together, but we had a laugh. Then we went out for dinner afterwards and had a great night. It did make me feel a bit weird, doors opening just because of who you were with. That said, I wasn't complaining!

* * *

As a family, we've been quite nomadic, we like moving around a lot. We've lived in a lot of houses. We've lived in Dubai, Surrey and now we're back up north where we started.

One thing I've realised is that it's never about where I live, it's really about where I'm at in my head because you can go on holiday, you can move around, but you take all your shit with you. I've done that a few times. When I've written about living in Surrey in the past, I just hammered it and hammered the people. I still think I've got a point but I think it was more about where I was at that time. I'm pleased I lived in Surrey now because at that time in my life, I was able to sacrifice Surrey. I was able to blame Surrey and the north-south divide. I pointed to the competitive culture and people and never took a good look at myself. If I'd experienced the end of my career while living up north, I wouldn't want to be in a position where I was blaming the North or where I'm from. I would have been ill if I found myself never wanting to return there, if that makes any sense.

When we moved to Dubai in 2009, I burned it as well. I just needed to get somewhere far enough away from reality, to escape my life for a bit, and Dubai was the perfect place at the time. But it had a really short shelf life. The work out there was alright, but the cost of living was madness – it's not good when you realise you're spending £30 every morning on a plate of fruit.

We got the memberships through for these gyms and I think I went once and never went back because it was so ridiculous. I'd go over to this skyscraper and the gym was right at the top. There was an attendant in the dressing room and as I was taking my clothes off, he was picking them up, folding them. Then, as I got in the gym, they were trying to put the weights on the equipment for you.

My clothes were washed by the time I came out and someone would be hanging around next to me dabbing the sweat off the floor every time I moved. It felt a bit claustrophobic and, especially coming from somewhere like Preston, it felt wrong having that level of supposed luxury.

Rachael has moved about a bit in her life too. We've been all over the world, and seen so many places, but the reality is we're edging ever closer to Preston, but it's taking a while. At the moment, all is good, the kids are really settled.

I've written some of this book on the banks of Loch Lomond, up in Scotland. If it wasn't for the midges in summer, I'd love to live in the countryside somewhere like that. It's strange how you get drawn to places in life – I've always liked to look out over water and I love the countryside.

I can't help but think about how the DNA test showed I'm 20 per cent Scottish. In normal circumstances I'm not into spiritual stuff, but I started thinking I might be a bit because even as a kid, I felt some connection with Scotland. I spoke to my dad about it and he's far from spiritual too, but as kids, we always came to Scotland on holidays and as a family, we were drawn towards it. We all speak about Scotland with an affection. My real name is Andrew after all, so maybe it was meant to be? Living on a loch, playing golf . . .

I bring the family to Cameron House in Loch Lomond, which is an incredible place to stay. In 2020, I was filming *Top Gear* all around Scotland and I absolutely loved it. I don't know what the pull was, but there is definitely something about it for me. My dad used to cycle all the time and when he was younger, he took his bike around Scandinavia. He also goes fishing in Norway every year, so maybe there's something spiritual in that 20 per cent Scandinavian and 20 per cent Scottish DNA.

I was in Iceland, and I know it's slightly different, but I loved it there. It must be the Viking in me. The cold, the mountains and the raw meat! I've been lucky enough to see a lot of the world and it's really weird because only two or three places have given me that feeling of home: the north of England, Scotland and a little bit of Scandinavia.

Thinking about it now, that's a life lesson. If you feel a connection with a place, I think you should listen to it. I often wonder how Florida would have worked out if we'd decided to stay in America when we were there in 2007 – I think we could have made a good go of it. Having said that, I'd never have forgiven myself for giving up on playing for England.

There's still time for another move (and we all know where I'm talking about). And I suppose that's true for everyone – there's still time. Nobody else can make the move for you. The strange thing is, since the age of 15, I toured so much, living out of bags and I've moved house 20 times. If I moved away, the times I've thought about it in the past, I'm sure I would have made a go of it, but the reasons were wrong. I was always running away from something: the pedalo, or injury, or the end of my career. My life was always all over the place.

I'm open to living anywhere, but it all depends on the kids now. I'm just going to follow them wherever they choose to go. I would never move for work, but I would live anywhere for my family . . . as long as it's Preston.

ACKNOWLEDGEMENTS

Thanks to Gordon Smart, Sara Drinkwater, Katie Lydon, Richard Thompson, Alita Butcher-Wallis, Clyde Holcroft, David Luxton, Liz Marvin, Matt Phillips, Madiya Altaf, Nikki Mander and all at Bonnier Books UK.

INDEX

AC Milan FC 94
academy cricket 85
achievement 5–6, 28, 59, 87, 110, 155, 166, 169, 200, 251
aggression 26, 36, 38, 42–3, 49–50, 55, 58, 171
Akram, Wasim 60, 75
Aladdin 129
alcohol consumption, *see* drinking culture
All Blacks 76
ALOTO, *see A League of Their Own*
ALOTO Road Trip 96, 128–34
alter ego 26, 37, 53
Aly, Waleed 98
ambition 36, 89, 99, 114, 155
ancestry 44–9
Anderson, Jimmy 78, 112, 152

'Andros Townsend Moment' 93, 94
anger 29, 41, 87, 109, 196, 237
Ant & Dec 44, 194
anxiety 87, 238
Arsenal FC 153, 172
The Ashes 77–8, 81, 99, 123–4, 135, 169, 178, 189, 197, 200, 219
aspiration 36, 70, 103, 150, 227
Atherton, Mike 54, 73, 83
Audio and Radio Industry Awards 199
Austin, Ian 13, 14
Australia 17, 29, 50, 81, 97–9, 105, 135, 181, 185, 200, 219, 253
autograph hunters 166, 195–6
awkwardness 35–8
Barker, Sue 106, 107
Barlow, Gary 176

Barnes, John 60–1, 95, 166, 203–4
Barrowman, John 141
Barry (neighbour) 20–1
Barrymore, Michael 173
Batty, Gareth 12
BBC 44, 97, 106, 113, 132, 141, 198, 239
Beadle, Jeremy 7, 171–3, 175
Beadle's About 177
Beaumont, Bill 107
Beckham, David 189, 218, 262
Bell, Andy 213
belonging, sense of 5, 13, 19, 32, 37, 143, 197
bidding wars 220–2
Big Bash, *see* T20
Bishop, John 89, 262
Blackburn Rovers FC 113
Blue 177
Blunt, James 98
bluntness 235
body image 4, 43, 53, 86–7
bonding 54, 130–1
Botham, Ian 108, 166
Bournemouth FC 46
Bowen, Jim 69
boxing 42–4, 134, 147, 149, 225, 249
bravado 104, 157, 237

Brisbane Heat 50, 97
British Home Stores (BHS) 72
Broad, Stuart 89
Brown, Chris 14
Bruce, Fiona 106
bulimia 87, 158, 196, 248–50
Bullseye 69
Bunbury CC 193
Butcher, Mark 143

Caine, Michael 171, 179–80
Cameo 204
Cameron, David 175–6
cancel culture 141
Caribbean Premier League (CBL) 186
Carson, Willie 107
celebrity interviews 179–90
Celtic FC 113
Champion Sports 226
Chandler, Chubby 89, 218
Chennai Super Kings 50, 220, 221
Chippendales 129–30
Christmas 68–70, 97, 124, 141, 194–6
Cinnamon, Gerry 3, 6, 8
Claire's Accessories 116, 148–9
Clarke, Darren 292
Clarkson, Jeremy 103, 110, 287–8
claustrophobia 251, 264

INDEX

clinical depression 241
coaching 13, 15, 40–1, 61, 75, 80, 84–5, 91, 96, 157, 174, 181, 200
Coe, Sebastian 132
Coleman, David 106, 107
comfort zone 37, 96, 238
community 27–32
competitiveness 19, 55–7, 103, 214, 263
computer games 58–9, 68–9
First World War 47
confidence 19, 35–63, 74–5, 87, 90, 95, 108, 117, 127, 139, 155, 174, 237, 242
Connery, Sean 93
cooking 204, 210
Corden, James 89, 90, 104, 128, 130, 131, 133–4, 176, 259, 262
Corden, Julia ('Jules') 176
courage 61, 88, 175, 190, 203, 248
Covid-19, *see* pandemic
Craig, Daniel 58
Crawford, Michael 139–41
Cricket AM 25
The Cricketers' Who's Who 166
criticism 53, 62, 91–2, 110–15, 117, 135, 150, 169, 236
Crouch, Peter 114–15, 138
Crown Paints 60–1

Daley, Tom 134
Davies, Gareth 107
Davis, Tom 125–6
Dawson, Les 173
Dawson, Richard 43
Day-Lewis, Daniel 43
DC United FC 153
De Niro, Robert 14
death 253–6
Debenhams 70, 71, 226
Dennis, Les 172
depression 44, 86–8, 154, 158, 161, 196, 237–45, 262 (*see also* mental health)
Derulo, Jason 180
Dickov, Paul 230
Discovery 129
diversity 28–32
DNA Journey 44–9
Do You Know What? (Flintoff) 281
Dott, Graeme 239–40
dressing-room culture 12–14, 19–20, 28, 32, 39, 52, 54, 60, 74–7, 90–1, 96, 104–5, 155–6, 168, 178, 196, 221, 241, 264
drinking culture 14–20, 26–7, 31, 45, 85, 127–30, 136, 144, 151, 157, 165, 168–76, 196, 213, 239, 245–8

drug culture 23
Du Beke, Anton 102
Dubai 50, 135, 263–4
Dutton Forshaw CC 12, 27
duty of care 16
Duvall, Robert 109
Dyer, Mal 28

eating disorders, *see* bulimia
ECB 166, 217, 218
Edmonds, Noel 173
ego 26, 37, 53–4, 112
Elizabeth II 175, 260
embarrassment 13, 46, 55, 100, 107–8, 187, 194, 198–9, 228, 238
encouragement 45, 75, 119, 195
England and Wales Cricket Board, *see* ECB
Ethiopia 292
Euro 2020 111
Evans, Chris 287–8, 292
Everton FC 94, 153, 252
The Exorcist 20–4

failure 147–62
fame 165–205
Fame, Georgie 193
fearlessness 36, 134, 152–3
Ferguson, Alex 155–6

'field goal kicking' 128
fighting, *see* aggression
finances, *see* money; taxation; wages; wealth
fitting in 12, 19, 22, 200, 235–9
5 Live, *see* Radio 5 Live 149
'fiver' anecdote 16–17
Fletcher, Duncan 200–1
Flintoff, Albert (great-grandfather) 45–7
Flintoff, Andrew ('Freddie'):
    ads work 194–6
    as awards host 203
    cars owned by 100–1, 109, 227–9, 290–2
    coaching qualifications 84–5
    DNA test 44–9
    'earring/tattoo' anecdote 115–16
    education 11, 15–18, 22–3, 35–40
    first cap 197
    first club contract 12
    grandfather's death 250–6
    as interviewer 179–90
    introverted nature of 138
    jewellery 116, 230
    Plan B 118–19
    podcasting 199
    singing 3, 4, 16, 25–6

INDEX

starting over 82–4
trainers collection 71, 100–1, 109, 115–18, 226–7
trophies/awards 51, 197–9, 203
wedding of 16, 135–6, 190–3
Flintoff, Christopher (brother) 24–7, 41–2, 60–1, 67–8, 71–2, 175, 255
Flintoff, Colin (father) 11–12, 20–2, 26–8, 38, 40–2, 49, 59–60, 74, 79, 99, 116–17, 250, 265
Flintoff, Rachael (wife) 28, 80–1, 97, 124, 136, 168–72, 179, 190, 201, 227, 230, 259, 264
Flower, Andy 80
Ford, Harrison 188–9, 204–5
Forsythe, Bruce 173, 194–6
Fox, Jason 95
Fraser, Angus 73
freedom of expression 117
friendship 123–44
fundraising 27, 134
Gallagher, Noel 26–7, 261
gambling 17
gamesmanship 55
gang culture 22, 30–1, 95, 210
'Gerald' interview anecdote 183–4
Gere, Richard 207, 230
Gervais, Ricky 235–6

getting-drunk anecdote 14–17
Glamorgan CC 11
Gooch, Graham 60
good manners 31–2
Gough, Darren 54, 82, 112, 143, 195
Gower, David 60
The Graham Norton Show 85
Grant, Hugh 182
greetings messaging 204
grief 236, 250–6
Guernsey 18
Gullit, Ruud 94

haggling 226
Hakkasan 130
Hammond, Richard 110, 287
'hanger' 87
hard graft 147–52
Hargreaves, Henry ('Harry') (grandfather) 250–6
Harmison, Steve 116, 151, 240–1
Harris, Calvin 130
Harris, Chris 105, 116
Head, Lee 38
Heart of Midlothian FC 113
Hello! 190–3
Henderson, Michael 73–4
Hendrix, Jimi 172
Hibernian FC 113

Hidden Side of Sport 239
Hilton, Martin 20–1
Holcroft, Clyde 96, 118, 132, 139, 267
Hollioake, Ben 253–4
Hollywood Ashes 189
Holmes, Kelly 132
Honey G 203
horror-movie anecdote 20–4
Hughes, Emlyn 107
The Hundred 87, 118–19
Hussain, Nasser 83

I'm A Celebrity . . . Get Me Out Of Here! 99
Ibrahimović, Zlatan 63
India 50, 124, 174, 220, 241, 254
insecurity 35–9, 52–4, 63, 108, 126, 191–2
international cricket 40, 50, 76, 89, 251
inverse snobbery 181
IPL (Indian Premier League) 50
Irani, Ronnie 13–14
Irwin, Steve 59, 117
ITV 44, 139

Jacamo 86
Jack Whitehall's Sporting Nation 132

James Bond (007) 57–8, 181, 229
JD Wetherspoon 210
jealousy 16, 109, 221
John, Elton 25, 163, 171, 177–9, 230–1
Johnson, Dwayne ('The Rock') 134
The Jonathan Ross Show 180, 187
Jones, David 115
Jones, Tom 179
Jones, Vinnie 262
Jordan, Michael 145, 155–6, 158
joyriding 23–4
JW Johnson 210

karaoke 16, 25
Kay, Peter 14
Key, Rob 37–8, 83, 116, 119, 143, 149–50, 203

LA Galaxy FC 262
LA Rams, *see* Los Angeles Rams
Lampard, Frank 179
Lancashire CC 11–17, 28, 31–2, 36, 39, 49, 52–3, 76, 85–6, 97, 137, 143, 158, 191, 197, 210, 214–18, 252, 289, 291
Las Vegas Raiders (Oakland Raiders) 128
The Last Leg 180
A League of Their Own (ALOTO)

INDEX

25, 55, 61, 88–96, 100, 103–5, 125–33, 138–9, 197, 237, 262, 288

A League of Their Own: European Road Trip, see ALOTO Road Trip

LeBlanc, Matt 103

Legal & General 101

Lewis, Denise 139

Lineker, Gary 112, 194

Liverpool FC 46, 60

Living with Bulimia 158, 248

Lloyd, David ('Bumble') 73–5, 83, 159, 215

lockdown, see pandemic

London Palladium 139–40

Lord's 59, 86, 143, 180

Los Angeles Rams 92

Lumley, Joanna 12–13

Lydon, Katie 159, 162, 181, 257, 287

McCartney, Paul 69

McCoist, Ally 107–10

McDonald, Trevor 174

MacFarlane, Seth 187

McGuinness, Paddy 104–7, 115, 292

McInnes, Donald 139

McKeown, Paddy (best friend) 39, 136–7, 212, 214, 223

Major, John 7, 171, 173–5

Manchester City FC 26, 73, 230

Manchester United FC 14, 84, 148, 153, 172, 252

Manford, Jason 262–3

Match of the Day (*MOTD*) 112

Matchroom Boxing 225

May, James 110, 287

memorabilia 196–200

mental health 47, 87, 255–56 (see also bulimia; depression)

mentoring 73, 159

Mercury, Freddie 23

Messi, Lionel 63

midlife crisis 115

mimicry 25, 105

Mind Media Awards 203

Minogue, Kylie 134

mistakes 20, 47, 135, 144, 152–60, 190, 214, 224, 247

Monday Night Football 115

money, value of 222–6

Moore, Roger 58

Morgan, Eoin 54

Morgan, Piers 170–1, 186

Morgan, Rupert 170

Morrissey, Neil 89

'Müller Vitality' anecdote 12–13

Muppets 88

Murphy, Stuart 91
Murs, Olly 101

naïvity 12, 23, 76, 166, 230
NASCAR 129
negativity 53, 117, 153
neighbours 20–1, 26, 212
Netflix 155
Neville, Gary 83
Neville, Phil 252
New Zealand 254
News of the World (*NOTW*) 168–9
nightmares 21
Norton, Graham 85, 189
nostalgia 71–2, 97

Oakland Raiders (Las Vegas Raiders) 128
Oasis 24, 26–7, 78
Ocean Colour Scene 24
Old Trafford 7, 11, 13, 28, 53, 59, 215
Old Trafford, Mr, *see* Pete
O'Leary, Dermot 115
Olympics 56, 58–9, 139
one-day cricket 54
'100' anecdote 150–1
The One Show 97, 114
online bullying 110, 111, 114

O2 Apollo 24
out-of-body experiences 26, 162, 188
The Oval 81, 174–5
Ovett, Steve 132

Pakistan 226, 241, 292
pandemic 110, 114, 248, 252
Panesar, Monty 78
paparazzi 170–3
parenting skills 4
Parkinson, Michael 93
Parrott, John 107–8
peacocking 51–3
peer pressure 21–2, 36–7
Persie, Robin van 172
Pete ('Mr Old Trafford') (groundsman) 7, 28–32, 259
Pickering, Mike 26
pick 'n' mix 67, 70
picture-taking culture 170–1, 197–200
Pietersen, Kevin 221
Pizzorno, Serge 78–9
Pogba, Paul 148–9
Ponting, Ricky 81, 185
post-traumatic stress disorder (PTSD) 47
Presley, Elvis 25, 69, 95
Press Club 168

INDEX

Preston North End FC 47, 108, 113, 213
The Project 97, 98
puberty 12–13
punditry 84, 110–15

Queen 23–4
A Question of Sport (*QoS*) 106, 107
Question Time (*QT*) 106, 287

racism 61
Radio 5 Live 149
Rajasthan Royals 220
Ramsay, Gordon 204
Ranganathan, Romesh 56, 104, 125–7, 132, 133
Rangers FC 107, 113
Rashford, Marcus 149, 177
Redgrave, Steve 132
Redknapp, Jamie 44, 46–7, 55–7, 61, 81–2, 89–95, 113, 116, 127–33, 203, 237, 259–60, 262
respect 16, 31–2, 41, 72, 76, 89, 112, 128, 165, 170, 211, 218, 231, 246
Rhythm Kings 193
Richard Thompson (agents) 89, , 162, 267, 287
Right, Said Fred (Flintoff) 283, 285–92

retirement 4, 15, 19, 38, 42, 55, 79, 89, 96, 104, 119–20, 135, 157–8, 188, 259
Richards, Viv 59, 166, 196
Ritchie, Guy 170
Rivaldo 218
Road Trip, *see ALOTO Road Trip*
Robbie, Margot 181, 185
Roberts, Dave ('Rooster') 86
Robinson, Lee 41
Robinson, Tony 139
Rogen, Seth 137
Rolling Stones 79, 193
Ronaldinho 218
Ronaldo 218
Ronaldo, Cristiano 63, 158, 214
Rooney, Wayne 148, 153, 172
Ross, Jonathan 180, 187
rudeness 72–3, 138
Ryan, Lee 177, 178

St Annes CC 119
SAS: Who Dares Wins 95–6
Satty Singh's 240
Savage, John 11
Savage, Robbie 199
Save Our Summer 114
school bullying 17, 22, 36–8
'Sea Life Centre' anecdote 180–1
selflessness 27, 54, 243

Seyfried, Amanda 187
Shearer, Alan 112
shoplifting 70
shrinkage 68–9
Sky 25, 55, 83, 89, 91, 113, 115, 118, 149, 225
sleepwalking 20
Smith, Graeme 150–1
Smith, Dave 20
Smith, Liz 20
Smith, Will 181, 185
social awkwardness, *see* awkwardness
social clubs 23
social media 3, 69, 94, 110–12, 117, 118, 148, 236, 254
Somme, Battle of the 47
songwriting 4–5
South Africa 17, 50, 150, 175, 177
'space hopper' anecdote 94
sponsorship 191, 221
sporting mentality 112
sports psychology 155, 157
Spriggs, Joy 32
Spriggs, Ron 32
Sri Lanka 168
Stan (fitness instructor) 141
Stanworth, John 13
Steele, Fraser 96, 126
Stewart, Alec 174

Stewart, Mickey 174
Stokes, Ben 87, 158
Stones, Mr (headmaster) 16–17
Strictly Come Dancing 102, 106, 195
Styles, Harry 117
success 147–62
Sugarhill Gang 95
Summerbee, Mike 73, 74
Super Sunday 115
superheroes 57–63
Swift, Taylor 130
Syed, Matthew 199

Tait, Sandy 47
Tajinder (friend) 135–6
talkSPORT 108, 110, 112, 148
Tarantino, Quentin 262
Taupin, Bernie 179
taxation 50, 161, 218, 220
team spirit 54
'tenpin bowling' anecdote 128–9
Test cricket 50, 59–60, 73, 78–81, 87, 116, 150, 168–70, 174, 179, 220
Theroux, Louis 101
Thomas Cook 127
Thompson, Daley 58–9, 166, 177
Thompson, Georgie 89, 90
Tokyo Joe's 41, 42, 71

INDEX

Top Gear 96, 103–7, 110, 115–18, 132, 149, 160, 229, 265, 287–92
Tottenham Hotspur FC 47, 94
touring 17–20, 240–1, 292
Townsend, Andros 93, 94, 238
tradition 50, 174, 248
Travel Fox 226–7
trolling 110–11
trust 52, 75, 126, 137, 142–3, 218, 220, 222–4, 247
T20 Big Bash League 97
Turner, Gabe 252
Tutu, Desmond 177–8
Tyson, Mike 60, 166, 203

under-11 cricket (U-11s) 16–17
under-14 cricket (U-14s) 36
under-15 cricket (U-15s) 11
under-18 cricket (U-18s) 40
United States (US) 128, 149, 201, 266
Vaughan, Michael 54, 150–2, 169
Vikings 44–9, 200–5, 265
vulnerability 35, 57, 236
wages 11–12, 67, 72, 84, 99–100, 166, 212, 215–20
Wahlberg, Mark 186–7, 190
Warne, Shane 181, 185, 198, 220
Watford FC 61, 179
Wayne (friend) 16
weakness 52–3, 157
wealth 123, 149, 160, 165, 200, 260
Weller, Paul 24
Wenger, Arsène 85
West Indies 28, 143, 220
Westwood, Lee 292
Wetherspoon, *see* JD Wetherspoon
White Tie and Tiara Ball 177, 179, 230
Whitehall, Jack 56, 92, 104, 128–34, 182, 189, 259, 262
Who Do You Think You Are? 44
Widdicombe, Josh 180
Williams, Andy 79
Woods, Laura 110
Woolworth ('Woolies') 7, 24, 26–7, 67–72, 99–100, 163, 166, 177, 189, 223
work mates 125–34
working-class values 24, 100–1, 225, 259
Wright, Ian 112
Wyman, Bill 193

The X Factor 203

Zarkana 129

DO YOU KNOW WHAT?

Are there aliens out there somewhere?

What happens when I die?

What's the worst that can happen?

Do You Know What? is an unexpectedly helpful, occasionally silly and absorbing brain dump on life and everything it holds, from one of Britain's most-loved national treasures.

OUT NOW

RIGHT, SAID FRED

Right, Said Fred is a much-needed Bible of straight-talking honesty and sharp observational humour: following an unprecedented time of collective global insanity, Freddie is ready to impart his effortless charm, wit and wisdom on a wild array of topics.

OUT NOW

IF YOU HAVEN'T YET READ

RIGHT, SAID FRED

read on for an extract from

CHAPTER ONE

CAR COMPETITION

When I heard that Jeremy Clarkson had been sacked from *Top Gear* for punching an Irishman, I got straight on the phone to my agents and said, 'I want to do that job.' They replied, 'Yeah, I can see it actually.' And I replied, 'Go on then, see what you can do . . .' Up until then, I'd kind of stumbled into everything. And out of all the jobs in TV, presenting *Top Gear* was the one I really wanted to do. That and presenting *Question Time*, but even I had to admit that unless every political journalist in the country was simultaneously wiped out in some freak accident, that was unlikely to happen.

Every idea I'd ever come up with, my agents Richard and Katie had managed to get me in front of the right people. But I'm glad they weren't able to work a miracle in 2015. Not that I was really in a position to take the job anyway, but taking over from Clarkson, James May and Richard Hammond would have been a poisoned chalice. Look what happened to Chris Evans when he started presenting the show – he got destroyed by the public and the media. I wasn't surprised. Not that I've got anything against Chris, but Clarkson had made that show his own. I'm not sure I'd want to be mates with him – or if you're even allowed to like him – but he was brilliant on *Top Gear*. How could he not have been? He made it one of the biggest shows in the world.

Three years later, I'd just finished filming an episode of *A League of Their Own*, which involved crawling through a muddy assault course in the studio, when my agent Richard wandered over with a big smile on his face and said, 'I've got some good news. But you're going to have to sit down.' I did as I was told and Richard said, '*Top Gear* have been on the phone and they want you to do a screen test next week, if you're up for it.' I didn't get too excited, because a screen test is just a trial, not a job offer. But I was bang up for it.

The opportunity had come at exactly the right time. I'd been thinking a lot about my TV career and whether I should do something else instead. I was still loving being on *A League of Their Own*, because I'd been doing it for eight years and grown so close to my fellow panellists, especially Jamie Redknapp and Romesh Ranganathan. But otherwise I was thinking about packing all the other TV stuff in. I didn't want to do anything I wasn't really interested in, so I was thinking about carrying on with *A League of Their Own*, doing some cricket commentary or presenting, and spending the rest of my time pottering. I enjoy being on TV and work hard at it, but it was never my dream and doesn't give me the same buzz as being a cricketer. Playing cricket for Lancashire and England was all I'd ever wanted to do. So I knew that walking away from TV work wouldn't be the same emotional wrench as retiring from cricket.

On a more basic level, I just loved cars. The car has got to be one of the greatest and most important inventions in history, right up there with the printing press, the light bulb and penicillin. The car is one of the few inventions that fundamentally changed the way humans lived, literally broadened people's horizons. Nowadays, people will try to make you feel guilty about owning a car, unless it's electric.

First, there isn't an electric car I like. Second, we don't have the infrastructure, in terms of enough charging points. Third, they're not actually that good for the environment. Yes, they produce less pollution, but making the batteries requires the mining of rare metals and a lot of extra energy. I'll need to have driven quite a lot of miles in my petrol car before it has the same environmental impact as a brand-new electric car. And because I change my cars quite a lot, I'm probably doing less damage to the environment than someone who drives an electric car. I'm not some knee-jerk reactionary who is against electric cars on principle, I'd actually like to get one eventually. But only when the cars get better, the infrastructure improves and it can be proved beyond doubt that driving one is better for the planet.

But whether you're into electric cars or petrol, gears or automatics, cars are such a big part of our everyday life that I struggle with people who say they're not into cars. They're lying. If you own a car and you drive a car, then you're into cars. You might not know anything about cars, but you're into them, whether you think you are or you don't. And I really can't get my head around people who don't drive. I can't even imagine it. When I was a kid, I couldn't wait to be 17 so that I could get behind a wheel. It meant freedom, being able to go wherever I wanted and do whatever I wanted. The reason I failed my test the first two times was because it was so important to me. The first time I failed on a dangerous (I thought there was more than enough room on the roundabout to get home, he disagreed). The second time I got a minor fault. As soon as I'd done it, I knew I'd failed. So I thought, 'I'm going to give him the ride of his life . . .' The third time I knew the bloke, which was nice. He played cricket for Morecambe and I used to play against him, so we talked about old times for 20 minutes before he said, 'You better do one of those emergency stops. If you want.' That was pretty much that, he passed me.

My first car was a black Fiat Uno, which I rented for a few months after passing my test (at the third attempt). Driving

CAR COMPETITION

it, I looked like one of the Ant Hill Mob from *Wacky Races*, because I could almost stick my arms out of the windows and pick it up. When you're a cricketer, you're always trying to get a car for free. Even to this day, I'm always trying to get free cars, it's just ingrained in me. My missus had a Kia Sorento for a while, because I got it for free. Don't get me wrong, it was a lovely car. But after a while she started asking questions, because it was usually parked next to my Ferrari. Back when I started playing, some of the older players had their names on the side of their cars: 'Neil Fairbrother – sponsored by Lookers'. I didn't want that, but Lancashire had a deal with Rover whereby I could rent one of their cars for 1 per cent of its value a month, plus about 30 quid for insurance. That worked out at about 150 quid a month. It's not as if they were going to let me have a 220 Turbo, so my first Rover was a 216 Coupé. I didn't drink at the time, so used to ferry my mates around on nights out. And every night without fail I'd get stopped by the police, because driving that car in Preston was the equivalent of driving a McLaren in Chelsea. I upgraded to a 216 cabriolet in blue, but there was obviously a mix-up, because when it arrived it was purple. So when I got a pay rise, I upgraded to a 620ti, which wasn't quite the stuff of Alan Partridge's dreams (I believe he drove a Rover 825), but not far off. Alas, someone went into the back of it when I was on my way to a game in Cheadle. On the bright side, I got a grand for the whiplash, taped the boot closed and carried on.

The first car I bought was a Porsche Boxster on tick when I was 21 (which came in handy on *Top Gear*, because one of the episodes involved us driving around Ethiopia in our first cars – Paddy had an Escort 1.6 and Chris had a Mini). I was on tour in Pakistan at the time and obviously feeling a bit bored and sorry for myself. When it turned up, it wasn't quite the colour I thought it was going to be. I knew it was going to be blue, but it was a bit brighter than advertised. But I loved that car, until one night I was driving down a country lane in Hale. It was quite icy, so I was taking plenty of care, creeping around these corners at 10 mph, when this B-registration Metro came hurtling towards me. I slammed on the brakes, but this Metro couldn't stop and hit me front on. It hadn't been going very fast – 5 mph at most – but the whole of my front end fell off. This Metro didn't have a scratch on it and its driver refused liability. So after that, the gloves came off.

My next car was a BMW M5, which came third-hand via the golfers Lee Westwood and Darren Clarke, who were part of the same management company. That car was a dream, unlike the Overfinch Range Rover I made the mistake of buying. I drove over a pothole and two wheels cracked, and when I drove through a big puddle (I promise it was nothing more than that), the undertray fell off.